Father and Son

Father and Son

A Personal Biography of
Senator Frank Church of Idaho
by His Son

F. Forrester Church

faber and faber
BOSTON • LONDON

To my mother

Designer: Mary Cregan

This book was set in 11-point Janson by the ComCom division of Haddon Craftsmen in Allentown, Pennsylvania, and printed and bound in the paperback edition by Fairfield Graphics, in Fairfield, Pennsylvania.
Published by arrangement with Harper and Row, Publishers, Inc. All rights reserved.

Library of Congress Cataloging-in-Publication Data

Church, F. Forrester.
    Father and son.

    Reprint. Originally published: New York: Harper & Row, c1985.
    Includes index.
    1. Church, Frank. 2. Church, F. Forrester.
3. Legislators—United States—Biography. 4. United States. Congress. Senate—Biography. 5. Unitarian Universalist Association—Clergy—Biography. I. Title.
[E840.8.C49C48 1987]   328. 73'092'4 [B]   86-24078
ISBN 0-571-12990-0 (pbk.)

Contents

Preface

The seed for this book was planted during a conversation with Schuyler Chapin and John Chancellor about a month before my father died. As we were having lunch in New York at the Century Club, I told Schuyler and John about my father's battle with cancer and the family decision to let him die at home. My great-grandfather Burnett died at home. I was only six years old but I remember it very clearly. It was not frightening. We kissed him good-bye and he died. Today more than ever before we are estranged from the inevitability and reality of death. We protect ourselves in ways that harm us. What once was natural, even sacred, has become a taboo. It struck me as something worth writing about.

As minister of All Souls Unitarian Church in Manhattan I am blessed by my congregation with a generous summer leave. My project for the summer of 1984 was to write a series of lectures I would deliver at Harvard Divinity School in the fall. For some reason they came easily and quickly. I sent them to Bernice Kanner, a sharp, clear writer, for her editorial advice. She told me to leave them as they were, suggesting that instead of revising them I invest the gift of newfound time in another way. I should expand the biographical and autobiographical fragments they contained into a book. I talked to Bernice on the fifth of July. By the end of August I had finished a draft, which I gave to Schuyler Chapin. He sent it on to Michael Bessie at Harper & Row. And that is the story of this book.

In addition to Cornelia and Michael Bessie and their assistant, Brooke Drysdale, whose advice was particularly helpful, four other people read my manuscript: Clayton Carlson, head of the Harper & Row religious books department, challenged me to describe the development of my faith in greater detail; my closest friend, Peter Fenn, who served my father as his chief of staff, saved me from many errors made in haste; my wife, Amy, protected me from myself with her tough but loving critique; and once again my mother, Bethine, forgave me my heresies and let me be myself.

This is a book about men, a father and his son. One woman is responsible, however, for much of the good that is in it. In fact, if there is a hero in this story—not a heroine but a hero—it is probably my mother. To her I dedicate this book with pride and love.

Father and Son

Introduction

One night not so very long ago, my five-year-old son, Twig, was unable to sleep. So he came to his father, who knows everything, and asked, "How can you sleep if you're not tired, Daddy?" I suggested that he lie in his bed and think of all the nice things that had happened to him during the day. That way, I thought to myself, I would not be responsible for any nightmares he might have upon being banished by his father to the lonely darkness of his room.

"Is that what your daddy told you?" he asked.

For the life of me, I could not remember what my father had told me on such occasions. In fact, I remember little from when I was a young boy. This led me to wonder whether my own son would remember me at all, not to mention the things I had taught him, if I were to die before he reached the age of five. Now I have a different problem: not that he will forget me, but that I will disappoint him.

My five-year-old son has enormous confidence in a father's ability to answer unanswerable questions. On my better days I try to disabuse him of this without crushing his childlike faith, but sometimes I take the path of least resistance. On this occasion, with renewed appreciation for my own parents, I nestled Twig into my lap, looked him straight in the eye, and lied.

"Yes, son," I said. "That is precisely what my daddy told me, and often it worked." There was a long pause.

"Daddy?" he asked.

"Yes, son."

"Why can't we see God?"

After a while you simply accept the surprising way in which a child's mind works. I thought for a moment and said, "That's a good and very hard question, Twig. I guess one of the reasons we can't see God is that God is everywhere. God is like the light from the sun on a cloudy day. We can't see the sun, but we know it's there because everything is light outside. Or God is like the wind. We can't see the wind, but we can feel it in our hair."

"Does God make babies, Daddy?"

What is one to do? It is eleven-thirty at night. I am minding my own business, and my five-year-old son asks me if God makes babies.

I started out well enough. I told him that God created life and gave life the power to keep on creating new life. The look on his face suggested to me that this splendid explanation was a bit too abstract, so I plunged into the details. Not all the details mind you, just a random selection of wrong ones.

I started talking about eggs. When a five-year-old asks you if God makes babies, think twice before getting into eggs. Before long we were talking about chickens. From hens and roosters we moved to yolks and whites, ending up somewhere between feathers and breakfast. I thought to myself darkly, he may never eat breakfast again.

It was very late. Right before he went to bed, Twig said to me, "Daddy, every day I want to think all the time

2

about the idea of God so that I can learn." He kissed me and went to his room.

I expect that one of the reasons Twig asks so many questions about God is that he wants to have serious conversations with his father. He knows that his father is a minister. On Sundays he attends church and hears his father talking about God. And so, when the two of us are together late at night and the opportunity for a serious man-to-man discussion presents itself, Twig often asks his father, or tells him, something about God.

There may be more to it than this. One of the most abiding images that we human beings have created for God is that God is our father or mother. The precise image differs according to the particulars of various traditions, but where God is known as creator, we know ourselves as God's children. When Twig asked me if God made babies, he touched upon a primary myth. We fashion our myths according to what we actually experience of life and death and love. When we read that "God so loved the world that he gave his only begotten son," we know from experience what that means. It is a projection of our own most intimate fidelity and vulnerability upon a cosmic screen.

The other reason that a father or mother image for God makes so much natural sense is that, initially at least, no other figure has such power over our lives, such all-encompassing knowledge and authority, as does a parent. In the biblical stories, God loves and judges and forgives us much as a parent might. God suffers with us and for us. God waits, sometimes patiently, sometimes impatiently, for us to grow up. God watches as we become lost in self-absorption. God weeps or rages when we forget or even reject the one who gave us breath, who loved us, who sacrificed for us time and again as we were coming of age.

In turn, just like our own children, as God's children

we respond sometimes with anger at our Father or Mother in heaven, sometimes with a deep sense of guilt or sinfulness, often with both. As both psychiatrists and theologians have pointed out, the story of the fall and many other stories from the biblical tradition are stories of generational conflict, stories of filial impiety, stories of a parent's blessing being bestowed or withheld or taken away.

"We can never know what God is," Twig said to me once. He is right, I think. That is one problem with the parental image. It is too familiar, too limiting. For me, God is not so much a father or a mother, but the genius of the life force, that which is greater than all and yet present in each. I do not pretend to know what this means. And I do not really care. God is the biggest word I know. Therefore, it is sometimes the only word that I can think of to use. Besides, or so I tell myself, anything that helps us to exult in and make some small sense of this blessed gift of life is divine.

I say this simply to warn you that what follows is, in a strange sort of way, a religious book. Religion is nearly as hard a word to define as God is, but if I were pressed to do so in one simple statement, it would be this: *Religion is our human response to the dual reality of being alive and having to die.* All religious beliefs and the actions stemming from them reflect an attempt, human and therefore imperfect, to make sense of life and death by finding meaning in both.

We are the only religious creatures on this planet. We are the only creatures who know they are going to die. That we know we are going to die not only places an acknowledged limit upon our lives, but also gives a special intensity, a special poignancy and moment, to the time we are given to live and to love. The very fact of death gives meaning to our love, for the more we love the more we risk losing. Love's power comes in part from

4

the courage that is required in giving ourselves to that which is not ours to keep: our spouse, children, parents, dear and cherished friends, even life itself. And love's power also comes from the faith that is required to sustain that courage, the faith that life, however limited and mysterious, contains within its margins, often at their very edges, a meaning that is redemptive.

Proverbially, the years of a person's lifetime can be measured as threescore and ten. By such a rule, the following journey spans half a proverbial lifetime—two lifetimes, really: the first thirty-five years of my life and the last thirty-five years of my father's. In reality, there is no such thing as half a lifetime, of course, save perhaps in retrospect. Even then the midpoint is often fixed by some other measurement than that of calendar years. If I should live on into old age, however, I would not in the least be surprised if the year I was thirty-five, the year of my father's death, marked the passage from one half of my life to the next. And thirty-five years ago, for reasons having nothing to do with me, my father's life changed so profoundly that the year of my birth might easily be viewed as the halfway point of his.

When I was six months old, my father was diagnosed as having terminal cancer. For over a year he had been having severe back pains, which he attributed to stress. He was newly married. He had just finished his first year at Harvard Law School, where he worked hard enough and did well enough to win early appointment to the law review. Ever since returning from China, where he served as an army intelligence officer during the Second World War, he had been in a great hurry to finish his schooling and establish a career. Back pain seemed to come with the territory.

The New England winter of 1948 was a severe one, with several great blizzards back to back. My parents lived in a little fourth-floor walk-up apartment on Hem-

enway Street in South Boston, and Dad commuted to
Cambridge. Their car was decidedly not designed with
Boston in mind. It was a baby blue DeSoto convertible,
which they had driven all over Mexico during a three-
month extended honeymoon that summer. Among the
car's more distinctive features was its hood ornament, a
shapely nude who lit up when the lights were on. In
pueblo after pueblo, people adorned her with flowers as
if she were a saint.

Boston treated my parents' prize possession less
kindly. It survived the hard winter, but was stolen on the
morning of my father's first final exam. Frank and Bethine delighted in that car. It was a symbol of their new life
together, and to have it taken from them was a personal
violation. But the year was over. They packed up their
things and traveled back to Idaho by train. Such was the
backdrop for my arrival on the scene.

My mother, Bethine Clark Church, an only child born
to her parents in their maturity, is a very strong-willed
woman. After one such year in Boston she was not about
to suffer another one, especially with her husband in ill
health and a baby on the way. So it was that Frank
sacrificed his newly won position on the *Harvard Law
Review*, and the two of them embarked for the more
gentle and familiar climes of Palo Alto, California,
where my father enrolled for his second year of law
school at Stanford.

I was born on the twenty-third of September, 1948. My
parents had found a little storybook house in Palo Alto,
and I am told that the sun shone down on my first few
weeks of life.

Things did not improve for my father. Throughout
the fall his back pains grew worse. Still, the cancer was
not detected until February, when he went into the hospital for what was originally to be a simple hernia procedure. My mother knew that something was amiss when

the one-hour operation stretched to six. Having discovered cancer, the doctors removed as much of it as they could. It had spread into his kidneys, and though they cut out glands in the groin, abdomen, and lymph system, there was no way in which all of the cancerous tissue could be surgically removed.

My father learned of his condition as he was coming out of anesthesia. After much matter-of-fact probing, a technician told him that the cancer was incurable and he would be lucky to live for three months. My mother was simply informed that her husband was in very bad shape after an arduous cancer operation and the prognosis was bleak. All she could think of was that she had waited through a war for him. He simply could not die now, not in this way.

Had Frank Church remained in the east he might very well have died that winter. As it happened, the Stanford Medical Center was sponsoring a radical experimental program in X-ray therapy, and his cancer was of an unusual type, very susceptible to X-ray. For six weeks, early every afternoon, he was burned with a megadose of radium. He would return home, play with his infant son, have a light dinner, and then get violently ill, fighting nausea as my mother read to him until, exhausted, he fell asleep.

My mother tells me that the reason she did not marry the first man who proposed to her was that she discovered she could not hold his head when he was sick to his stomach. With my father it was not that way at all. Throughout his illness, she held his head night after night. In the meantime, I was platooned off to a series of great-aunts, old friends, and neighbors. By no means did I languish. My mother says that I was the picture of contentment. Judging from photographs in the family album, if contentment and baby fat are synonyms this surely was the case. I was one of those rotund little babies who seem even happier than they are because simply to look at them makes you laugh. As I grew round and pudgy, my father wasted away. By springtime his six-foot frame carried only one hundred pounds, but he was alive and the cancer was gone.

Shortly after my wife, Amy, and I were engaged, my parents took us to The Shadows, a restaurant in the hills of San Francisco, where they had gone some twenty years before to plan what little was left of their future together. They told us that on that evening they decided that they would leave me with my grandparents, go to Italy, choose some perfect spot in Sorrento, and drive off a cliff together. I doubt that they would actually have done this, but they might have. My parents shared a romantic temperament, in my mother's case decidedly Latin, in my father's more Germanic, and they were passionately in love. Besides, they had no real fears where I was concerned. All four of my grandparents were living, and my parents knew that I would be well cared for. In a matter of days, the question was moot. They arrived at the hospital one morning and a doctor, who my mother says looked like God, told them that the cancer was responding remarkably well to treatment. My father would live.

It was the third time Frank Church had been saved by modern medicine. He was rescued at birth by an emergency cesarean section following major complications attending his delivery. Later, as a boy, he almost died of a series of acute bronchial infections, only to be saved by the advent of penicillin. And now, what once would have been incurable cancer proved to be susceptible to the power of the latest advances in medical technology.

The doctors did caution him that, given how potent and extensive the radiation had been, his system's natural ability to combat disease was diminished and some ten to fifteen years would likely be taken off his life.

8

According to the odds as listed on the mortality tables, however, this would give him a good thirty or forty more years. As he observed years later, "I had previously tended to be more cautious, but having so close a brush with death at twenty-three, I felt afterwards that life itself is such a chancy proposition that the only way to live it is by taking great chances."

For twenty-four of the thirty-five years remaining to him, Frank Church served in the United States Senate. He authored legislation that has preserved millions of acres of American wilderness and kept a dozen wild and scenic rivers running free. He was an early opponent of the Vietnam war. He directed the most extensive investigations ever to be mounted of multinational corporations and the CIA and FBI. He had a brief fling at the presidency in 1976. He was floor leader during the bitter fight for ratification of the Panama Canal Treaties. And he closed his career in the Senate as chairman of the Foreign Relations Committee.

In 1980 Frank Church was defeated in his bid for a fifth term. Three years later, when he was fifty-nine, cancer struck again. He was not destined to beat the odds a second time. In April of 1984, after a brief, hard illness Frank Church died at home in his bed unencumbered by mechanical life supports. My mother lay by his side. As my five-year-old son, Twig, said to me on the day of my father's funeral, "God is not the only one who lives forever, Daddy. Love lives forever." I know that he is right.

My father was a third-generation Idahoan. My son and daughter are native New Yorkers. My father's life is now over. Theirs are just beginning. In so many ways, my own life seems poised in the balance between. One reason for this, I suppose, is that the birth of a child or the death of a parent alters our position on the ladder of mortality. Nothing changes really. Life remains just as fragile as it ever was, both our own life and the lives of those we love. It is simply that our perspective changes when a child is born or a parent dies.

In addition, there exists a special bond between father and son, even as there does between mother and daughter. Often for a man, his struggle for identity is to some extent at least a contest with the image of manhood he knows best, that of his own father. Judging only from my own experience, in large measure this contest is fought within. He strives to become like or unlike his father by fashioning his own life accordingly. As he comes of age, however, often the struggle is more open and can be very painful. At stake is his freedom, or so it seems. It is as if he is not free to become himself until he is tested against his father on some field of judgment. Yet even then, the object is not simply to best his father and establish independence, but also to win his father's blessing. Accordingly, the goal of such a contest is twofold: at once to vanquish and to be blessed.

At another level the bond between father and son, as with mother and daughter, is almost transpersonal—that is to say, suggestive of some elemental reality or figurative likeness. One generation precedes another all the way back to the beginning of time. If our lives were reduced to the barest of particulars, we each would be known, as distant ancestors are, by the vital statistics on a family tree: name, sex, date of birth, date of death, father's name, mother's name, and, if we marry, the name of our spouse and the names of our children. That is all.

In recent years, awakened to consciousness by the feminist revolution, more and more women are openly acknowledging their bonds with one another not only as sisters but as mothers and daughters as well. In part, their example inspires this book. It is a book about fathers and sons. I write as the son of a father and the father of a son. This is my only source of authority. As to why I am writing, my father has just died and my son is growing up. If anything matters, such things as these must matter. They are the basic, common human things we share.

As I write these words it is early July. I am in Boston, living for the summer in the First Church parsonage, a grand old town house at the top of Chestnut Street on Beacon Hill. My mother has just stopped through on her way back from Maine. Secretary and Mrs. Muskie had invited her to Campobello to celebrate with them the centennial anniversary of Eleanor Roosevelt's birth.

"Dad and I always held a special fondness for this city," she said. "After all, it is the place where you were conceived."

I walk our children to their summer school through the Boston Garden and down Marlborough Street. They ask me one question after another, most of which I cannot begin to answer. "Daddy, how many presidents are there in the world?" "Why can you sometimes see the moon, Daddy, when it is light outside?" "Is Opa in heaven, Daddy?"

As we walk along the garden path, I answer their questions as best I can. Each hints deep within at some great mystery that none of us can ever know or name. We walk along hand in hand, talking about the sex of ducks or what makes it rain, and I am reminded once again of what they too may discover one day. The whole thing—this strange business of birth and love and death —is nothing less than a stupendous miracle.

I. Idaho

1871-1957

My father and my son and I all bear the same name, as did my father's father and his father before him. It was first given in 1850 to the last of six children, a boy born in Cherryfield, Maine, to a mill owner and his wife. Since then the name has been passed down from generation to generation. It is not the birthright of the firstborn male, however. My father is the second of two boys, born nine years later than his brother, Richard.

When our first child was due to be born, Amy hinted broadly that we would exercise our opening option toward breaking the century-old tradition of naming at least one male child after his father. Following a certain amount of friendly argument, I was ready, perhaps too ready, to relinquish at least as much ground as my grandfather had. I promised Amy that if our first child did turn out to be a boy, we would name him whatever she wished. For instance, she had a great-grandfather named Samuel. My opening gambit, a tongue-in-cheek suggestion that we name our son Frank Forrester Church V and call him Sam, was quite properly dismissed, so we set out in earnest in search of a new name.

One thing seemed certain. It would surely be a boy. In all the years since the birth of Great-aunt Eva over a century ago, with but one exception there had only been boys born into my father's side of the family. Perhaps this is one of the reasons so many of my relatives made their careers in the military. After all, traditionally the military has been a male bastion. One great-uncle and his son were both admirals. My uncle Dick went to Annapolis and was a career officer in the Marine Corps. His son Scott attended West Point and for several years served as a lieutenant in the U.S. Army. We even number a CIA agent in our family. All of this makes Frank Church's political heresies, his opposition to the Vietnam war and his investigation of the intelligence services, all the more remarkable.

I was in the delivery room at New York Hospital on September 20, 1978, when our baby was born. The doctor prided himself upon being able to identify the sex of an infant before there was any hard evidence upon which to base a scientific claim. "Delicate ears," he said. "Yes, it looks like you have yourselves a girl." As the doctor congratulated us on our newborn daughter, one of the attending nurses had the presence of mind to look more closely. "Doctor," she whispered. "Come here a minute, please." I was terrified that something was amiss. "Well, what do you know," he exclaimed. "It's a healthy little boy!"

A few minutes later the delivery team was gone, leaving us alone to cradle our new son. "Well, Amy," I asked her, "what shall we name him?" She hesitated for a moment, then smiled and said, "I guess we had better stick with Frank Forrester Church V."

Amy sensed how much it meant to me to bear my father's name. Not all of it was positive. With a name come certain expectations. Those expectations are often hard to fulfill. On the other hand, I can remember as a very little boy, when all I knew about him was that he was my father, how proud I was that my father and mother had named me after him. I can remember thinking how amazing it was that, almost exactly a century before, another little Frank Forrester Church was growing up, learning his letters, playing with his friends. There is an intimacy about sharing a name that binds one somehow more closely to another, even across the years.

For my son, all of this has proved somewhat confusing. His name is Church. His father works at a church. He attends church school on Sunday, and nursery school at the church during the week. Add to this the fact that he carries the same name as his father and grandfather, and what you end up with is either a somewhat mystical sense of the intimate connectedness of all important things or a major identity crisis at a very early age.

I hope my son will understand that in naming him what we did we were in no way attempting to shape his destiny. At least we will try not to do this. Even so, by its own weight his name may sometimes prove a burden for him to carry. To the extent that it does, he may discover that burdens are not altogether bad.

After we had decided to name our son Frank Forrester, the nickname came to us much more easily. My nickname had been Twig, and so Twig it was.

As Twig will learn as he goes back in the family records, he was born into a long-standing, if not particularly distinguished, American line. My father was fond of pointing out—and fortunately the lesson was not lost on me—that the secret to whatever success we may enjoy is that we marry well. Of those bearing the Church name, our first American ancestor, Richard Church, arrived in Boston without conspicuous prospects in 1630. Shortly thereafter he moved to Plymouth, where he met and married Elizabeth Warren, whose father had come

over on the *Mayflower*. The Warren family was a prominent one in the colony. Richard, unfortunately, had a
roving eye and, if family lore is to be trusted, a penchant
for Indian maidens. His wife, therefore, was the foundation stone of the family, which, if never distinguished, at
least became serviceable. The children and their heirs
moved from town to town in New England, building
mills and producing lumber. By the fourth generation
they had settled in Cherryfield, Maine.

Frank Forrester Church, the last of six children, was
born on July 7, 1850. He was educated at Cherryfield
Academy and Bangor Business College. When he was a
boy, his older brother Albert's wife died, and Albert, like
so many other young men of that time, decided to make
a new life for himself in the American west.

Following his brother's footsteps, Frank Church set
out on his own journey westward in 1871. The spring of
that year he arrived in Placerville, Idaho, and went into
the lumber business with Albert. The local economy
turned on gold and silver, however, and so in 1875 he left
Idaho for San Francisco to study mineralogy and assay-
ing. Returning to Idaho the following year, he settled in
Idaho City and assumed a position at the Boise County
Bank and Assay Office. In May of 1881, he married Mary
Elizabeth Barry, whose family were early pioneers in the
Boise Basin.

Idaho City, a picturesque town nestled among the
pines in a river basin some twenty miles north of Boise,
had once been a boom town. At the height of the gold
rush in the early 1860s it is estimated that as many as ten
thousand people may have lived there. In 1864 an ob-
server noted that Idaho City had nearly sixty saloons and
half as many stores. Well before Frank Church arrived,
the town had fallen on hard times. In the winter of 1865,
the snowfall reached a depth of seven feet. There was a
bread shortage that spring, followed by a raging fire that

began in the dance hall and destroyed nearly every building on the city's two major streets. By 1878, when Frank
began his new career there, the population had fallen to
less than half its boom-town size. Almost a century later
his grandson was to return to Idaho City, now almost a
ghost town, to declare his candidacy for President of the
United States.

The first Frank Church was also the first member of
our family to enter politics. Building upon his experience at the bank, he decided to run on the Democratic
ticket for county treasurer in 1882. He lost to the local
postmaster, but tried again four years later and was successful. During the middle of his second term, in 1893,
President Grover Cleveland appointed Frank Church
assayer in charge of the United States Assay office in
Boise. He served his constituents well. The local paper
reported in 1893 that he was so well respected as an assayer that a miner often took gold to him without weighing it to be "smelted, assayed and run into bars, such was
his confidence in his integrity." Church and his family
lived above the Assay office in a stone building at the
corner of 2d and Idaho. It stands in downtown Boise to
this day. My great-grandfather died two years before my
father was born. The date of my father's birth was July
25, 1924.

My grandfather, Frank Forrester Church, Jr., was
born to Frank and Mary Church in 1890. Raised and
educated in Boise, for a short time he attended Gonzaga
College, but had to return home on account of his health
and never went back. In 1913 he married Laura Bilder-
back, a third-generation German-American and a se-
cond-generation Idahoan, and went into a business as a
sporting-goods store owner. This made their young sons,
Frank and Richard, the envy of the neighborhood. Every
Fourth of July, their father would gather up all the un-
sold fireworks from his shop and take the boys and their

friends to the foothills above Boise. There they would set off the most glorious display in town.

My grandfather Church was a Catholic, as his mother had been. Also, as was appropriate for a small businessman in Boise, he was a good Republican. The only time he voted Democratic was in 1932, when he cast a vote for Franklin D. Roosevelt against Herbert Hoover. He never forgave himself. On election day in 1936 he and my father wept as the election returns came in proving Roosevelt a landslide victor over Alf Landon. Judging from all the sunflowers—Landon's trademark—sported on lapels in downtown Boise, neither of them could imagine how he possibly could have lost.

Frank Church retired early from his business and ran a small apartment building in Boise, before coming out of retirement during World War II to oversee the local rationing program. With two sons in the military, he felt it his duty to make some contribution to the cause. The position he assumed was not an enviable one. My father always felt that the strain of two sons overseas and hundreds of plaintiffs daily on his doorstep broke my grandfather's health and shortened his life.

My grandfather died of a heart attack in 1950 at sixty years of age. I was only two years old when he died, and I am not really sure that I remember him. I think of him, however, as a modest man without great ambition. As unpretentious as he was private, my grandfather Church was the sort of person who preferred to smoke at night because he liked to see the smoke rings curl in the lamplight.

In one respect, however, Frank Church could be quite contentious. He had what my father once described as a "propensity for getting involved in awkward political controversy." One thing my grandfather loved with a passion was a good political argument. The habit was catching. From an early age my father discovered that the best way to get into a dinner table discussion was to champion the New Deal. He would often go to the library and prepare his case carefully in advance, just to see if he could best his father in the next evening's debate.

On one political point the two of them agreed. Senator William Borah, chairman of the Foreign Relations Committee and the Lion of Idaho, was their great hero. From long before my father was born, Borah, a Republican, had served in the United States Senate. His interest in foreign policy powered my father's own. There was something grand about a son of Idaho playing a major role on the national and international political stage. It was proof of what this country at its best was all about, equal opportunity based upon merit. My father and grandfather were proud of Bill Borah. He made them proud of Idaho and therefore proud of themselves.

When he was fourteen years old, Frank Church decided that his great goal in life was to become, like Borah, chairman of the Senate Foreign Relations Committee. He told this to his best friends, Carl Burke and Stan Burns. He could not have chosen a more receptive audience. They upped the ante to President and there in his kitchen on Franklin Street started plotting his political future.

This was done not wholly out of loyal boyish enthusiasm. There was already evidence of Frank Church's natural gift for statecraft. In 1938 the Boise *Capital News* invited letters in response to the question "Should the United States keep out of foreign troubles?" William Borah, by that time a leading isolationist, had recently warned the United States to "beware of warmongers." The local paper was interested in knowing whether local opinion matched that of their controversial senior U. S. senator. Young Frank, then an eighth-grade student at North Junior High School, sent in a reply defending his champion. Not only did the paper run it on the front page of their evening edition, but several letters to the editor were received expressing disbelief that a fourteen-year-old could possibly be responsible for such a tour de force. The paper had to publish a letter from Frank Church's social studies teacher attesting to the fact that the whole thing had not been a practical joke.

Frank Church left the Catholic Church and the Republican Party at about the same time, his freshman year in high school. Well trained by his father in the art of original thinking, he had become skilled in forming his own ideas, testing them not only at the dinner table, but in any forum available to him. Soon he was Boise High's champion on the debate team. It was not simply a matter of being a large fish in a small pond. He went on to compete in the national American Legion oratorical contest, and, successful in the local and regional competition, he bested his peers in the national finals. First prize was a scholarship to the college of his choice.

The importance of the American Legion scholarship cannot be overestimated. Frank Church's family was not poor, but neither did they have much discretionary income. For him to go to school out of the state, not only would his brother have had to repay, as he did, the family loan that made it possible for him to cover secondary expenses during his years at Annapolis, but money that was not available would need to be added to this in order to cover the tuition and living expenses at a school like Stanford. The four-thousand-dollar scholarship was therefore a necessary boon, making it possible for him in the fall of 1942 to move to the San Francisco Bay area and begin his college career.

However important winning this scholarship was, it did not mark the most critical turning point in my father's young life. That took place in 1940, when Chase Clark was elected governor of Idaho.

Chase Clark had moved to Idaho from Indiana at the age of two. His family settled in Mackay, under the shadow of what is now Mount Borah. At a very young age, campaigning stylishly in the first automobile in the county, Clark won election to the state legislature. Upon marrying Jean Burnett, the granddaughter of a Mormon bishop who had come over from Scotland and joined Brigham Young in his pilgrimage west, he, with his wife, homesteaded Robinson Bar Ranch, a seventy-acre property which had served as a stage stop since 1890. It lay in a charming little valley along the Salmon River some sixty miles from Stanley, an hour's drive from what is now Sun Valley. Resting above a natural hot spring, the location was ideal for a dude ranch. Taking advantage of this, Chase and Jean built two swimming pools, one of them a natural hot water spa.

During my childhood, I spent every summer at Robinson Bar. One of the reasons that it was so splendid a place to grow up is that one could try almost anything without suffering the consequences. When we were 13, my best friend, Jimmy Bruce, and I went through the trash cans one afternoon and mixed every drop of liquor we could find into a single concoction that left us reeling. There was no place for us to reel except into a wildflower field where we were discovered by my great-aunt and put directly into our beds.

Every summer I spent three months at Robinson Bar. In the daytime we would fish and ride horses. In the evening we would gather by the fire and sing songs or tell stories. At night, when due to radiational cooling the temperature would drop to near freezing, we would cavort in the 110° hot spring pool, returning to our cabins impervious to the cold. Robinson Bar was a kind of paradise.

I am sure that my parents appreciated their freedom from children in the summer, but they rarely enjoyed the same sort of vacation that I did. Much of their time was spent campaigning, riding in parades, and going to county fairs. Many politicians take their children with them to such events. Parades in particular provide great photo opportunities.

Robinson Bar left the family in 1972. Frank Church had just authored legislation that established the Sawtooth National Recreation Area. This included in its compass a large area in the White Cloud mountain range, which in part touched upon our property. Church was one of the first senators to make full voluntary disclosure of his financial holdings. He felt that even the appearance of a conflict of interest should be avoided by public officials. So we sold Robinson Bar for a pittance. Today it is owned by singer Carole King.

Bethine Clark was born in 1923. Because Jean Clark had lost a child—and almost her own life—due to primitive hospital care in Mackay some ten years earlier, as soon as she conceived again, Chase arranged for a short-term position as a lawyer with the land bank in Salt Lake City. He commuted to Mackay throughout the fall and winter to attend to his home practice. My mother was born in February. As soon as Jean was strong enough, the family moved back to Idaho.

Five years later, Clark suffered his first major setback. Due to a highly successful law practice, he had come to own the better part of Stanley Basin. He would accept land in exchange for legal services. In addition to his law practice, he had become a trustee of a major local bank. Clark's fortune was lost in the crash of 1929, when the bank closed its doors and he personally made good on every small claim for the return of invested funds. He managed this by selling all of his land with the exception of Robinson Bar.

Although he was no longer wealthy, Chase Clark's success in politics continued. He moved to Idaho Falls in

1932. Shortly thereafter, he was elected mayor. His brother was elected governor of Idaho. And in 1940, after an intervening term, to avenge his brother's defeat Chase Clark himself ran as the Democratic candidate for governor and was elected. He and his family moved to Boise, the state capital, and Bethine enrolled in Boise High School as a senior.

Frank Church and his politically precocious friends lost no time in making the acquaintance of the governor's daughter. Before long their regular after-school meeting place had moved from the Church family kitchen to the kitchen of the governor's house. By midyear Frank and Bethine were "best friends." She stayed in Boise for her first year of college to be near him as he completed his final year of high school.

The most promising opportunity in Chase Clark's political career failed to materialize because of his defeat for reelection in 1942. In 1941 Franklin D. Roosevelt had begun to look west for a running mate to replace Vice President Henry Wallace. Wallace was to the left of Roosevelt on many key issues. Roosevelt decided that he needed a new westerner on the ticket in 1944, and began to survey possibilities.

One day Governor Clark got a call from the White House. He was to be picked up early the following morning by an air force plane and taken to an undisclosed location to meet with the President. In my study I have a picture of the two of them sitting in a car on the shoulder of a highway somewhere in the state of Washington. Roosevelt told Governor Clark of his dilemma. They agreed to keep in touch over the coming three years, and Chase Clark returned to Idaho with the dream of the vice-presidency dancing in his head.

Because of war fever, 1942 was a Democratic year. The only Democratic governor not to be reelected was Chase Clark of Idaho. He had been a very popular governor and was considered a shoo-in for reelection. Early in 1942, however, a Catholic priest came to him pleading for some action to address the growing problem of overcrowding at the state penitentiary. There were nearly three times as many prisoners as the penitentiary would hold. Murderers were sharing cells with pickpockets. Representing an interfaith delegation of clergy, the priest suggested that the only solution to this crisis of overcrowding was for the governor to pardon all those who were unlikely to repeat the crimes for which they were sentenced. Clark set up a commission, and within three months of election day pardoned over one hundred prisoners. Only two ever returned behind bars—several were even present at his funeral in 1966—but the issue for which his opponent had been searching presented itself with a vengeance. Chase Clark was responsible for letting common criminals back on the streets. He was defeated by fewer than two hundred votes, and two years later Senator Harry S. Truman of Missouri was chosen by Roosevelt to be his running mate.

The Clarks became Frank Church's second family. It was Chase Clark who provided Frank Church with a living example of politics as something more than an abstract discipline. Not only did they share, as Frank did with his own father, a passion for politics, they also shared the same convictions. Years later Church's first success in the political arena can surely be attributed in no small measure to Chase Clark's influence.

In early 1942, just before Clark was defeated in his bid for reelection, Frank Church began his college career. His initial stay at Stanford was brief, but not without significance. He joined the Stanford debate team as a freshman. Inspired by this success, and powered more by ambition than good sense, he promptly dove into campus politics. Twenty-five years later as a freshman at Stanford I was to make the same mistake.

My father's cause seems trivial in retrospect, but it mattered deeply to him. The issue was freshman representation in the student governing body, at that time a radical notion which no one had even thought to consider. Even Frank Church's old friend and fellow freshman Carl Burke, who had gone with him from Boise to Stanford, was as embarrassed by the cause he embraced as by the zeal with which he pursued it. A breach was formed between them that was not repaired until after the war.

I received much kinder treatment. By the time I entered Stanford in 1966, freshmen had a place in student government. I myself was a member of the Student Council. Only one hurdle remained. We were not yet running it. Setting out to right this injustice, when an opening occurred during my first quarter at Stanford I leapt into the breach and ran for student body vice-president. On the basis of a distant second-place finish in a field of five, the following spring I was tapped as part of a dream ticket—Business School student and freshman, two hitherto neglected minorities—which fared no better in the regular elections than I had done before.

With the exception of antiwar activities, I took only one more brief fling at student politics. More than anything else it was a lark, the counter-culture equivalent of a fraternity prank. In my sophomore year I was the campaign manager for a topless dancer who based her campaign for student body president upon her body. This proved to be a remarkable though not unbeatable platform. Her stock speech was delivered to the accompaniment of music. To the cheers of enthusiastic audiences, she removed her clothes. There is no question but that my own limited education in this regard was decidedly advanced during the course of this brief campaign, but it ended any aspirations I might have had for further success in student politics.

By that time, however, the world and my views were in such dramatic flux that I had already decided to withdraw from the fray, repairing to a little bungalow in the foothills above Stanford. There I began to search for some deeper truth than I had known before.

My father's abortive career in student politics also ended by choice, but by a very different choice than I had made. He was saved from the wrath of upper classmen, the retreat of his old friends, and the relative meaninglessness of campus politics by the Second World War. In early 1943, at eighteen years of age, midway through his second quarter at Stanford, Frank Church enlisted as a private in the U.S. Army.

Contrasting my father's college years with my own, nothing stands out in starker profile than the difference in effect, not only upon us but upon the entire country, of our two wars. My friends and I, protected in large measure by our student status, considered burning our draft cards; my father and his friends, wholly unprotected, did not wait to be drafted—they joined up. If you had asked either of us at the age of eighteen what the motive for our action was, each of us would probably have said "Peace." The difference is that he wanted to make the world safe from Hitler and Tojo. My friends and I wanted to make the world safe from Lyndon Johnson.

This difference represented far more than a simple breakdown in patriotism over the intervening years. It represented a deeply felt if often naive and half-articulate response to our country's loss of mind and soul. The Second World War united us at home and expanded the circle of our influence abroad. The Vietnam war accomplished the very opposite. It divided us at home and led even our closest allies to back away from us. As for my friends and me, not unlike my father and his friends a quarter of a century before, we too were struggling for something in which to believe. The difference is that we could not find it on the battlefield that had been chosen for our generation to fight and die upon.

After boot camp at Fort Ord, Frank Church was transferred for additional training to Lafayette College in Easton, Pennsylvania. Years later as a U.S. senator, Church was to return to Lafayette to receive an honorary doctorate. Back then he was an eighteen-year-old private studying Spanish. As Frank wrote to Bethine in July of 1943, "Just where we Spanish students will fit in is not clear. We are studying the geography, history, economics, etc. of France, Italy, and Germany, nations to be occupied after the battle ends. But what is in the offing for Spanish linguists, nobody knows. Probably not even the government!" Years later the Spanish Church had learned would serve him well. As it turned out, however, over the short term it would have been far more useful for him to have been taught a smattering of Chinese.

Upon completing his training, Church, now a private first class, was notified that he would be sent overseas to the European theater. Just days before he was to embark, he and two others were reassigned to the military intelligence school at Fort Ritchie. At eighteen, Church was by far the youngest man in the program. The training was intense. "I am spending fifteen minutes each day 'taking it easy and relaxing,'" Frank wrote in response to one of Bethine's still favored instructions. "May I think of you when I relax?" After a few months at Fort Ritchie, he was promoted to corporal and sent on to Officers' Training School at Fort Benning, Georgia.

In March of 1945, Church was on a troop transport ship, zigzagging through the treacherous waters of the Pacific on his way to India. "I find it hard to believe, on so beautiful a night, that enemy submarines hide beneath these quiet waters awaiting their prey in hopes for a sudden kill. The whole of the universe—with all its magnificence, cold and barren—seems to look down and mock our puny impudence, our senseless savagery."

Lieutenant Church was officer in charge of perhaps the smallest Order of Battle team in the Second World War. It consisted of Church, Technical Sergeant Bill Emerson, who was later to publish the *Saturday Evening Post* magazine, and Staff Sergeant Nathaniel Pennypacker, scion of one of Philadelphia's first families, whose grandfather had been governor of Pennsylvania during the period of Teddy Roosevelt's reign in the White House.

On April 6, Church and his team arrived in New Delhi. Within a month, the three of them were traveling over the Burma Road in a jeep toward China. Their destination was Kunming, the capital city of Yunnan Province, in the "Valley of Eternal Spring." "Nature carved out China on a wild and lavish scale," Frank wrote Bethine. "All along the road, high above the tiny valleys and wind-swept plateaus, the barren mountains rise in stern magnificence."

Until the war opened the Burma Road, the people of Kunming had had next to no contact with the outside world. Now Kunming was a headquarters for the Chinese Combat Command. In June of 1945, Frank wrote to Bethine of his first encounter with a comparatively large group of young Chinese: "Although they had studied English in the universities and understood it fairly well, [they] had never before spoken to an American. Some were frightened. All looked upon any American with mixed feelings. But after the ice was broken, they began to show interest and spirit. My capacity for diplomacy was put to a severe test when several asked at once 'Why should the British be allowed to take back Hong Kong?' Now there, Bethy, is a good question!"

Church's responsibility was tracing the movements of

enemy units, together with making new identifications and estimating enemy strength. In Church's citation for the Bronze Star, it is recorded that "these studies were so well prepared that intelligence agencies made requests for additional copies and language personnel in the field used the special studies as chief guides in interrogations. Aside from this Order of Battle work, First Lieutenant Church gave daily presentations to the Combined Staff sections, which were so unanimously acclaimed that the Commanding General personally commended him."

The commanding general, General McClure, discovered Church almost by accident. Major Tussman, Church's immediate senior, had been giving the G-2 estimate at the daily morning full-staff conference. He was temporarily called away. Church was invited to make the presentation, and McClure was sufficiently impressed to make the private suggestion that Church continue to officiate. Accordingly, when the forward echelon of the headquarters moved to Chinkiang, where preliminary arrangements were being made with the Japanese for the final surrender at Nanking, Church accompanied McClure as the acting G-2. When it came time for the surrender to take place, Church was one of the American representatives to witness the ceremony in Nanking. "Someday," he wrote Bethine, "if I make no mark elsewhere, some Chinese historian will run across my signature on the memorial roster, buried among those of the other guests who were invited to attend. I felt like a member of the chorus, high upon the platform backstage, in one of the finale acts of history."

By now Church and McClure were quite close. The general held a dinner party to introduce the young lieutenant, proclaiming Church to the other six people present—all colonels—as "the man with the finest diction in the army." During the course of the evening McClure asked Church to read aloud one of the general's favorite stories. It made him feel like a court jester, but also led to an invitation to accompany the general on a special trip to Hangchow, which turned out to be Church's most fabulous experience during the course of the war.

"There were only three in the American party, the General, his aide-de-camp, Captain Owens, and I. We joined General Ho Yin-chin, Supreme Commander of the Chinese Army, and his staff at the airport. We flew to Hangchow in Chiang Kai-shek's personal plane, and there the festivities began.

"That evening we attended a dinner of honor given in an auditorium in the middle of the city. It was an Oriental feast I'll long remember. If numbers matter, there were between nineteen and twenty-four courses, fresh shrimp, cracked crab, roasted duck served in its own broth, spiced chicken, sweet and sour pork, swordfish stomach, and countless other delicacies I couldn't possibly name, let alone remember.

"The banquet over, we returned to the Governor's place for dancing. Left were only twelve of us in the party, and we found upon our arrival twelve very lovely girls from the city's best families. The dance lasted until midnight, being interrupted for hot coffee and French pastries at hourly respites.

"But the evening was far from over. Hangchow is both the Niagara Falls and Venice of China. Her West Lake, filled with gondolas, is the honeymoon Paradise for the fortunate newlyweds who can visit the city. And, therefore, the evening had to include a trip on the lake. We were rowed out to an island of lotus blossoms, resplendent in the phosphorescent glow of the harvest moon. I told the Mayor that I should like to spend my honeymoon in Hangchow on the lake, and he assured me that if I would telegraph ahead, he would come to Shanghai and welcome me. . . . He's a grand fellow, and showed us a wonderful time . . . The Mayor and I, if you can imagine, sang 'Strawberry Blonde' and 'I Want a Girl Just Like the Girl that Married Dear Old Dad' all the way back to the Governor's palace. Bethy, it was like a tale from the Arabian Nights."

Frank Church's letters to Bethine Clark from China are rich in local color, historical detail, and political commentary. Because of his position, plotting Japanese troop movements and analyzing the progress of competing units in the Chinese Army, he was able to study the beginnings of a gradual shift of power which would eventually lead to Chiang's downfall and Mao's ascension. His year in China also gave him a firsthand perspective on Asian politics that he would draw upon in the early 1960s as he formulated his own grounds of opposition to our growing involvement in Vietnam.

Writing from Shanghai in December of 1945, Church observed, "The coming of peace and the return of the Chungking government, ironically enough, have served to aggravate more serious problems. Inflation, bad enough during the war, has become progressively worse during the past three months. The housing shortage is acute as a consequence of the arrival of large numbers of Chinese and American troops. The municipal government is practically impotent, and akin to its big brother, the national government, notoriously corrupt. It seems capable of nothing other than throwing its weight around by imposing exorbitant taxes, and enforcing annoying curfews. Chiang is fast losing prestige among the people."

One of Chiang's weaknesses, my father later told me, was that he became trapped by the allure of the West. A Christian who valued Western customs and manners, he and his inner circle slowly lost touch with the pulse beat of China. Mao was out in the provinces with the peasants, scorning foreign influence and preaching a gospel that, if also in its own way a foreign import, he had shaped to the contour of indigenous aspirations. Even during the year that Frank Church was in China serving in the joint staff of the Nationalist high command, Mao and his lieutenants were winning the hearts of the people. It was only a matter of time before Chiang's government would fall.

Though commentary such as this is the stuff of which most of my father's war stories are made, I do recall one anecdote that indicates his tour of duty in China was neither without its moments of adventure and danger, nor without occasional moments of levity. As often was the case with my father's stories, this vignette spared no expense when it came to his own dignity or pride, but it is amusing.

One day, as he and his Order of Battle team were traveling along the Burma Road accompanying a Chinese Army convoy, a disturbance was heard in the valley below. The immediate fear was that they had been discovered by the Japanese. Church was the ranking infantry officer and, therefore, the officer in charge. Immediately, the new commander leapt into action.

A stream lay parallel to the road they were on. Both correct military tactics and common sense suggested to the young lieutenant that he should command his troops to dig in across the stream and wait in this protected position for the enemy. As this maneuver was being carried out, Lieutenant Church discovered that his rifle was jammed, clogged with the dust and dirt of the road. It was dusk and so he climbed under a truck, covered himself with a heavy blanket, and to the light of his flashlight cleaned his rifle. By the time he had finished this operation, it was dark outside. If he were to attempt to cross the river and rejoin his troops, they might mistake him for the enemy and fire on him. Frightened and chagrined, Frank Church thus spent that night by himself under a truck on the other side of the river from his troops. They, fortunately, believed that he, courageously, was acting as their sentry. Even more fortunately, the Japanese turned out to be a drunken band of Chinese soldiers. Within a week, Lieutenant Church had led his convoy safely to its destination.

At the end of his tour of duty in China, First Lieutenant Frank Church was awarded the Bronze Star. Later he was inducted into the Infantry Hall of Fame in Fort Benning, Georgia. Church returned to Stanford in 1946. By taking double the regular course load, a year and a half later in the spring of 1947 he earned his bachelor's degree, majoring in political science. He also won the distinguished Joffe medal for debate, and graduated Phi Beta Kappa.

While at Stanford in 1946 and 1947, Church was often on the local lecture circuit speaking of his experiences in China. People were looking for a patriotic travelogue. What they got was a damning indictment of the Chiang regime. Before Frank Church knew it, again he was in the middle of a controversy.

In January of 1947, Frank reports to Bethine, "I weathered through a minor crisis in the Speech and Drama Department down here last week. I had been invited to give the keynote talk at the Toastmasters' Club in Redwood City tomorrow evening, and had accepted on the understanding that I would deal freely, and without restriction, on the Chinese situation. When I learned later that the talk was to be a 'travelogue,' and that it was intended to be 'neutral and non-controversial in nature,' I withdrew my acceptance, and suggested they invite another in my place. This brought on a series of conferences which ended with the decision that I could speak on my own terms. I think this will hold for the rest of the year, and I'm glad to have the matter favorably and finally settled. One of the chief reasons, I think, that we will never avoid that final act of horror, an atomic war, is simply because whole societies are caught up and held fast in a spasm of timidity. Even our most liberal and advanced colleges quake at having the fragile myths attacked. They would rather see them laid open for dissection in the 'hush-hush' chambers of the private conference room."

In February, Church crowed with pleasure at the feathers he had ruffled by his blunt assessment of the situation in China. "The well-fed matrons of San Jose, where nothing disturbing has occurred in the last decade, are pleasantly aroused by my teapot tempest on China, and they have taken whip in hand to prod their husbands into line. This has led to a splash of invitations recently which has turned me professional. Yesterday the Rotarians paid me twenty-five dollars for a half-hour talk. Taking money from the Rotarians is practically as worthy a cause as damning the regime of Chiang Kai-shek. If I can manage to get things well enough organized, perhaps I'll be able to buy a dress suit for our wedding."

Frank and Bethine married on the twenty-first of June at Robinson Bar. Away from Idaho for the next three years while Frank went to law school, they did return during the summers, and Bethine remained in Boise during the fall of 1948 when I was born. In 1950, following my father's recovery from cancer and the completion of his legal training at Stanford, the family moved back to Boise, where we were to live for the next six years.

We lived in a little house on Logan Street. My father's best friend, Carl Burke, having also finished Stanford Law School, moved in next door. Logan Street was a cul-de-sac, one block long and almost wholly free of traffic. It was ideal for unchaperoned children, and a merry band of us thrived there.

Our house itself was tiny, and made even more so by

my parents' color scheme. I can remember the living room and my parents' bedroom very clearly. The former was painted, walls and ceiling both, forest green. With only one west window, there was no way to light the room so that it would appear to be anything other than a grotto. In contrast, the painter who mixed the paint for my parents' bedroom had painted the wall the color that my mother had intended for the trim. Her original scheme was bad enough, but when the entire room was painted shocking pink rather than baby pink with shocking pink trim, the results were electrifying.

I think I can honestly say that all of my early memories are happy ones. I can remember popping tar bubbles in the driveway on hot summer afternoons. I can remember playing endless hours in a little wading pool with Chris Burke and Jimmy Bruce, my other next-door neighbor and for years my closest friend. I can remember trips to the drugstore to buy little plastic packets of miniature cowboys and Indians. There were birthday parties. There were family vacations. And once I even got to stay home from school for a whole month when I had chicken pox, measles, and mumps back to back. In all, my early years were unremarkable and very pleasant.

I did take my share of bruises. For one thing I was not a "tough kid." My mother used to hide behind the curtain and watch with pain while one particular friend of mine would beat me up. Finally, she could not stand it any longer. "Twig," she said, "he's smaller than you are. If you just hit him once he'll stop."

"But I can't hit him, Mother," I said, with tears in my eyes. "I'm not mad at him."

Throughout these early years of my life, Frank Church was laying the groundwork for his political future. In 1952 he was elected chairman of the Idaho Young Democrats. That same year, he and Carl Burke ran for the state legislature in Ada County and lost. This was the sum total of his experience in running for elective office when in 1955, at the age of thirty-one, he tossed his hat into the ring as a candidate for the U.S. Senate.

The Republican incumbent at that time was Senator Herman Welker, a protégé of Joe McCarthy's. Despite the fact that Idaho was a Republican state, Welker had been badly hurt when McCarthy fell from favor. Church judged 1956 to be a particularly promising Democratic year.

He was not the only one. He entered a field of four other candidates, all of them more seasoned and experienced. The most prominent among them was ex-Senator Glen Taylor, a cowboy populist who had retired from the Senate to run for Vice President as Henry Wallace's running mate on the Progressive ticket in 1948. Notwithstanding his left-wing politics, Taylor had an avid following in Idaho. He and his family were a kind of traveling medicine show. On the stump, Taylor would sing and play his guitar, and his wife and children would accompany him. His greatest moment of national visibility had come when he rode his horse up the United States Capitol steps.

Though huge in size, Idaho was then a state of fewer than half a million people. If one had sufficient energy and time, it was possible to shake the hand of a fair percentage of the electorate. Frank and Bethine campaigned door to door for nine straight months. Given the cost of elections today, their effort would have been impossible. They sold their "half a house" for $6,000 to finance the primary. The total cost of the primary was just under $14,000.

I moved in with my grandparents, Judge and Mrs. Clark. This is not the only contribution they made to my father's election. Despite his own vigorous efforts, Frank Church would likely not have had a chance against the better known and more seasoned field he was competing against without the advice and influence of Chase Clark. Clark had not fallen from view following his defeat for reelection as governor in 1942. President Roosevelt had appointed him federal district judge for Idaho. In addition, his nephew, David Worth Clark, had been the last Idaho Democrat to serve Idaho in the U.S. Senate and was Herman Welker's predecessor there.

As the primary results came in, Frank Church and Glen Taylor were locked in a dead heat, with Church holding a scant 50-vote lead when the initial tally was complete. When it became clear that the final returns would not be known for many days, Chase Clark packed the family up and took us all off for a vacation at Lake Tahoe. With every morning's news the tally changed. It was like living on a roller coaster. One day we would be 300 votes ahead, the next, 75 behind. Two weeks later, however, when all the votes were finally counted, Frank Church was the victor by 170 votes. He returned to Boise triumphant, the only hitch being that I had left my favorite stuffed animal at our motel. At my grandfather's insistence, we turned around, retraced the one hundred miles we had already traveled, and rescued him.

Compared to the primary, the general election turned out to be relatively easy. Admittedly, there was no support for the top of the ticket in Idaho. In a straw poll taken in my third-grade class, only two of us voted for Adlai Stevenson. When we were asked why we supported Stevenson, my compatriot said that he was Stevenson's cousin. As it turned out this was not true. He was simply embarrassed and looking for a good excuse. He never wore a Stevenson button again. This prompted me to ask my mother for a bigger one.

Following his defeat, Glen Taylor moved to California and went into business manufacturing "Taylor's Toppers," a successful line of men's hairpieces. He did not reconcile himself to Church until the 1976 presidential campaign, when, still true to his old radical politics, he buried the hatchet and supported Church on account of his work as chairman of the Senate Intelligence Committee.

Herman Welker met a sadder fate. Shortly following his defeat for reelection to the Senate, he died of a massive brain tumor. During the campaign it had seemed at times that Welker might have had a drinking problem. On occasion he would slur his words and seem to lose his train of thought. Certain of Frank Church's supporters recommended during the course of the campaign that he find a way to capitalize upon this. On one occasion, sixty thousand much needed pamphlets outlining Welker's record and alluding to the fact that he had been known to fall down on the Senate floor were donated to Church's campaign. They had a big inkblot on the front cover, and over it the words "The Shameful Record of Herman Welker." Prevailing over the protest of his aides, Church refused to use it. He asked Porter Ward, one of his staff assistants, to burn the whole lot in the back alley, insisting that he stand by the incinerator until every last one of them was turned to ash.

In December, the thirty-two-year-old senator-elect and his family moved to Washington. This begins the next part of my story, but let me close this chapter with two things that I remember very clearly from our first month in the nation's capital. The first is the inaugural parade. The second is a gift my father gave me.

My parents had what I thought was a particularly wonderful car. It was a red and white 1952 Kaiser. We called it the Tahitian delight, because it had fake-straw plastic interior trim. It had been their campaign car. They had painted "Church for Senate" on it in big blue letters, surrounded by stars. I was sad when they repainted it after the election was over. My father was always loyal to his cars. During the years he was in

Washington, he had only three: this Kaiser; a 1957 Ford; and a 1965 Mustang convertible, which he drove for the final twenty years of his life and gave to my brother shortly before he died.

On January 20, 1957, my parents and I headed downtown in our Kaiser to watch the inaugural parade. The only problem was that we did not know where we were going. My father had just put on his new "U. S. Senate" license plates, and so every time we came to a barrier the traffic officer would simply wave us through. All of a sudden, there we were right in the middle of Pennsylvania Avenue. Both sides of the street were filled with people. Up ahead of us was the reviewing stand, and two blocks behind us we could hear the drums of the Marine Corps Marching Band and see the President's car. We were leading the inaugural parade, and there was no way out of it. My parents slumped down in the backseat. I was in the front with a young staffer. I could not have been more proud. My father told the driver to find some kind of escape. He dropped us off right in front of the reviewing stand, saying, "Senator, it's a brave thing for this little car to do."

The other thing I remember is far more important. When Frank Church was sworn in by Vice President Nixon to the United States Senate, he was presented with a number of gifts, some from the Senate itself. One of these was something that had been presented to members of Congress since 1904. It was a little book called *The Life and Morals of Jesus of Nazareth* by Thomas Jefferson.

I had read bits and pieces of the Bible before, of course. Having attended Presbyterian Sunday school on occasion, I was acquainted, in broad outline, with its principal characters and plot. Admittedly, it was the coloring book approach to the Bible in which I was most thoroughly versed. And whatever I might have gained from this in religious depth and commitment was further limited by my appalling lack of artistic talent. I knew enough not to color Jesus blue, but had a terrible time keeping the sky out of his face. It was not until my father presented me with my very own Bible, all words and no pictures, that things began to happen.

As it turned out, the Bible that my father gave me was a very peculiar one. As I later learned, Thomas Jefferson, near the end of his first term in the White House, excerpted from the four Gospels his own version of the teachings of Jesus. It opens with Mary already great with child, no mention being made of any extraordinary circumstances surrounding the conception. It closes with an account of Jesus' crucifixion, death, and burial.

What an extraordinary revelation for a nine-year-old boy who knew how the story was supposed to turn out. The resurrection was missing. This story, the tale of God's son, Jesus, who preached salvation and announced the inbreaking of the Realm of God, ended in the all-too-human way: having for a brief time lived, even having loved and served so well and so memorably, the hero died.

My father told me that this was the way he understood the story of Jesus. For us, who were born in the usual way and shall die in the usual way, it is Jesus' unusual life here on earth that really mattered. Jesus was not special because he happened to be more than human or other than human. He was special by virtue of how fully he managed to realize the promise of his humanity.

When first reading Jefferson's Bible, I had no idea either that Thomas Jefferson had Unitarian leanings or that I myself would grow up to be a Unitarian minister. But I do remember what my father said to me that day about religion. He quoted Thomas Jefferson. "It is in our deeds and not in our words that our religion must be read."

2. Washington

1957–1966

It is difficult to describe a happy man. My father was one of the happiest men I have known. There was nothing austere or forbidding about him, at least when he was among his family. As I was growing up my father and I had basically a dinner table—and game table—relationship. We played catch together only once and it was embarrassing for both of us. At the dinner table, however, we engaged in a refined form of locker-room repartee. At first, he was much better at this than I. But both of us expressed our love for one another by means of the elegant put-down.

Relaxation and enjoyment were the code words in our household. For my mother particularly, having fun was almost an article of faith. "What's wrong?" she would ask me across the dinner table. "Nothing is wrong, Mother." "Then why aren't you smiling?"

If it is hard to smile in response to your mother's cue, it is also hard to have fun when your father seems fated to embarrass you in public. When we ate at restaurants, my father almost always ordered rare roast beef. Every time, right before he put his fork in for the first bite, I would brace myself and inwardly cringe—this might just be the time he would moo. Dad had the best, most startlingly preternatural bellow I have ever heard. It began somewhere deep within, his lips and eyes closed, with a low-pitched "mmmmmmmmmm" and then he would open his mouth and, moving toward the treble register in a crescendo, would utter an ungodly "aaaaaaAAAAAaaaaa."

My father also slid down banisters in public places. When you are ten years old and trying to seem grown-up, there is nothing more mortifying. Once he lost control and crashed into the door of a doctor's office across the hall from the stairs in the lobby of a building in Boise. We ran down the stairs after him. Before we got there, a nurse opened the door. She started to pick him up. When she recognized him, she put him back down on the floor, blushed, and said, "Oh, excuse me, Senator, I didn't know it was you."

The other thing my parents did that embarrassed me was sing in the car. Whenever we went anywhere they sang things like "Let Me Call You Sweetheart." Even when no one else is listening, that sort of thing is acutely embarrassing to a prepubescent boy. Amy and I don't have a car, so I sing in the elevator. Nina is still young enough that she can laugh. Twig blushes to the ears and kicks me in the shin.

I had one recurring nightmare when I was a boy. My father and I are driving together on a winding road spiraling up a steep mountain. We pass by half-familiar landmarks, people, and houses. Occasionally someone calls out. Dad smiles and waves. Higher and higher we climb, my father singing, into the clouds. I am filled with a rush of excitement but also with dread. And then, suddenly, a logging truck or some other ominous hurtling vehicle swings around the bend into our lane. We swerve and plunge off the cliff. Falling. Darkness. It seems like an eternity. And then, just before we crash against the rocks, I wake up. My fear was not for myself. It was for my father, reckless, buoyant, unconcerned, beautiful, singing as we plummeted toward our doom.

When we first moved to Washington my parents rented a house on 44th Street, and I was enrolled in the third grade at Horace Mann School. We did not stay there long, but during the six months I attended Horace Mann I was in a mixed third-fourth-grade class with Julie and Tricia Nixon. It had not yet and would never fully dawn on me that I was anything special, either advantaged or disadvantaged, for being a senator's son. I brought this same lack of understanding or presumption to my appraisal of my two apparently famous classmates. All I remember is that both of them were very nice, especially Julie. Tricia, however, was part of the fourth-grade contingent. I expect she found it a matter of pride to distance herself as much as possible from third-graders like her sister and me.

Many people, themselves victims, have spoken of how difficult it is to grow up in a politician's household. I do not mean to question their sincerity. It may indeed have been difficult growing up where they did. It can be difficult growing up anywhere, even in a privileged environment.

I have no memory of anything being particularly unusual about my upbringing, although for the first four years that my father was in the Senate, my schooling was split between Boise and Bethesda. This did prove difficult at times. I had two sets of friends, two houses, and two completely different images. In Idaho I was a star, a straight-A student, the top of my class in almost every subject. My school in Idaho, however, was about half a year behind. During the first semester, the one spent in Idaho, we would cover the same academic ground that we had in the last semester of the previous year, the one spent in Washington. This was all very good, but the obverse was not. I barely passed fourth grade, ending up with three C's and three D's in the six major subjects. Over the next two years, with the help of tutors, I managed to become a solid C student, but this was after the "gentleman's C" had gone out of fashion, even in elementary school.

One other thing about my upbringing, something that I was oblivious to at the time, is that all of the discipline came from my mother. It was not that my father could be prevailed upon to let me do things that my mother would not let me do. It is simply that I can remember no occasion when he was called upon to punish me or volunteered to do so on his own. I am sure that the same was true for my brother, Chase.

Chase Clark Church was born on September 20, 1957, near the end of our first year in Washington. He was the answer to many prayers. After the extensive exposure to X-rays that Frank Church endured at the time of his first battle with cancer, he was left not impotent, but sterile, and thus unable to father any more biological children. Upon returning to Idaho in the early 1950s, my parents decided to adopt a second child. They received word on September 20, 1957, just before my ninth birthday, that my brother had been born. He was the best birthday present I ever had.

Chase had a milk allergy which we were late in detecting, causing him to spit and sputter with great energy. This led our parents to nickname him Sput, which we lengthened to Sputnik when the Soviets beat us into space later that fall. Sputnik, however, was not a useful nickname for the son of a senator already suspect for his liberalism. Our mother is fairly credited as being the great political genius of the family. When asked one day by a reporter why we called the baby Sput, she corrected him by saying that Chase's nickname was actually

"Spud." Not bad for an Idaho baby. With children named Twig and Spud in a state known for its forestry and potatoes, the bases were covered.

Spud brought tremendous joy into our house. As far as I can remember, I felt no competition. The nine-year difference in our ages meant that neither he nor I tended to get into one another's hair as we were growing up.

From an early age, my brother proved by nature and temperament to be an outdoorsman, a real child of Idaho. I never took much interest in hiking, climbing, or trailbiking, and certainly not in hunting. The closest I ever got to a gun was when my fifteen-year-old brother tried in vain to teach me how to shoot skeet. He, however, was a natural in everything having to do with the outdoors: rods and guns, tents and backpacks, horses and trails, woods and streams.

As Chase was growing up three things happened that might have made it more difficult for him to enjoy what he loved best. The first thing was that the Senate had moved gradually to a year-long session. This meant that schooling in Idaho was out for him. The second was that our father came into his greatest period of prominence just when Chase was entering adolescence. And the third thing was that in 1972 my parents sold Robinson Bar Ranch. As I look back on it—and Chase concurs in this —what our parents did to compensate for these three things is really quite amazing. They rented a cabin, a little Civil War vintage cabin in Fairfield, Pennsylvania, about ten miles from Gettysburg. Every other weekend they went there with my brother and his friends. For years there was no phone, and they did not accept Friday night or Saturday night social engagements. Instead they fished with him, walked the mountain trails, visited the battlefield, taught him how to shoot a gun.

When in Gettysburg, Frank and Bethine Church were far, if not totally, removed from the Washington world.

One attraction to certain of their friends was that the cabin was on a particularly fine trout stream. One day, just as the family was about to pack itself off to Pennsylvania, British Ambassador Sir Peter Ramsbotham called. He, Justice Potter Stewart, and Secretary Elliot Richardson were going to be fishing the stream that Saturday and wondered if they might drop by for a visit on their way home. This led to one of my brother's favorite stories.

Ramsbotham, Stewart, and Richardson did not arrive until after dark, wet and hungry after a full day of unsuccessful fishing. My mother had anticipated this and had thrown together a pot of cabin stew, which was simmering on the stove. In the tiny cabin—one room serving as kitchen, dining room, and living area—the three men got into an involved and animated discussion, which began to extend well into the evening. Finally, the four of them were impressed upon to come to table. As they sat down, with a particularly sweeping gesture Elliot Richardson flourished his paper napkin into the candle flame. The napkin ignited. Richardson is one of the few people in politics who speaks in complete sentences, and he was in the middle of a very elaborate one. So without dropping a phrase or compromising a clause, hardly in fact even looking down, he dropped the napkin in his plate, picked up his knife and fork in European fashion, and proceeded unperturbed to put out his napkin as if he were cutting a piece of meat into very small pieces. Chase and his friend Johnny Kimelman politely excused themselves, went upstairs, and buried their heads under pillows. You could feel the ceiling shake, they were laughing so loud. Downstairs, the conversation continued without Elliot Richardson's ever mentioning his burning napkin.

It is said that Frank Church was not a member of the club. There is no question but that this is true. It was not that he had no use for it. He enjoyed the company, the camaraderie, the late-night cloakroom conversations while awaiting votes in the Senate. It was simply that he had little time for it. Particularly with Chase, but also as I was growing up, he and my mother were careful to seize as much free time as they possibly could, that they might be there for us.

During my father's memorial service at the National Cathedral in Washington, I said that Chase and I were raised not in the home of a great man, but rather in the home of a great father. Things seemed to be in their proper place, and we were secure in our parents' love. If my children can say as much of me, I shall account my own experiment in fatherhood an unqualified success.

I had few "serious" discussions with my father when I was a teenager. Our relationship was light and filled with banter. My father relaxed at home. We spent almost all of our time together in the pursuit of enjoyment— although there was one very sober discussion, my classic, obligatory introduction to sex. Not that I knew that this was happening, because at the time I didn't have the faintest idea what my father was talking about. Admittedly, I was not a terribly precocious or advanced thirteen-year-old. On the other hand, he could not have been less clear. He came into my room one evening and said, "Forrest, one of these nights something may happen to you, maybe in your sleep after a dream, which you will not fully understand, and when this happens I want you to know that I will be very happy to talk to you about it." "Sure, Dad," I said. That was it.

I did get a few glimpses of my father at work in the summer of the same year, when I served as a Senate page. Even then, however, I was concentrating not so much upon him as upon me. There is no one more cocky or self-important than a Senate page. For three months, I negotiated the corridors of power, impressed tourists, made fun of senators' idiosyncrasies, and flirted with receptionists. I especially relished the hour before the Senate went into session. Tours of visitors were rotated through the galleries while, below, we would move officiously from desk to desk, setting out the previous day's *Congressional Record* and the schedule of legislation. The tour guide would say, "The Senate pages are now preparing the chamber for today's business." It was grand.

I drove back and forth to the Senate with my father in his '57 Ford. He was lost in thought, not at all the same person I knew from home, and we traveled in silence together. I felt like a little man.

When Frank Church arrived in Washington in 1957, at thirty-two years old he was the youngest United States senator. Even then, he looked far younger than his years. Among the letters of condolence I received following my father's death was one from the wife of the man who built our house in Bethesda. She remembers first meeting my father while putting finishing touches on the kitchen the day before we were due to take possession of the house. He walked in wearing Levi's and a Pendleton shirt. She said to him sharply, "Young man, I do not know why you are here, but I am very busy at the moment getting this house ready for a United States senator who is going to move in tomorrow, so I will have to ask you to leave." Shortly thereafter she recalls taking us for an afternoon swim to the local country club, where he was asked by the lifeguard to leave the pool when the appointed hour came for grown-ups to have exclusive use of it.

Frank Church remained boyish in appearance throughout most of his life. I can remember one family vacation during my college years when I had a long, somewhat unkempt beard that at the time I considered fashionable. We went out for dinner together one evening. I was presented with the check. Years later, when

47

I was moving into a new apartment in New York, the doorman was delighted to discover that my brother was the famous Frank Church.

There were many jokes that traveled the cocktail party circuit in Washington concerning Frank Church's youthful appearance when he first became a senator. And it was true that he had to give up wearing blue suits, because people, including other senators, mistook him for a page boy. One day a woman came up to two young men standing by an elevator in the Capitol. "I understand that one of you page boys gets mistaken for Senator Frank Church." "Yes, ma'am, one of us often does," Senator Church replied.

Frank Church was typed by the press as a "boy wonder." It was a hard thing for him either to grow out of or to live down. Because of his training in formal debate, he was also dubbed, often in unflattering tones, the "boy orator." This was to lead to his first big break, the keynote address at the 1960 Democratic Convention. It also was to contribute to his image as one who was in love with his own voice, stilted and pretentious, pompous and grandiloquent. These epithets were to dog Frank Church throughout his entire career.

The keynote address itself was a very mixed blessing. On the one hand, I have met hundreds of people who saw Frank Church on the television that night and have never forgotten it. People still tell me that it was one of the greatest speeches they have ever heard. And in its own way it was a stirring speech. It was a set piece, however. Filled with the cold-war rhetoric of the time, and loaded with stock rhetorical phrases, it had something about it of the textbook address.

In a way, Frank Church overprepared the event. He went over his speech again and again. He refined it until its every cadence rang clear. One problem that he had was outside of his control. It was the first convention

48

with the modern teleprompter, which Church had never used and did not need. He said to the convention manager that he did not want the teleprompter. This fell on deaf ears. The result was that throughout his speech, when he added a line or skipped a phrase, the operator would frantically roll the text backward and forward. Church had refined his speech up to the very moment of its delivery. Accordingly the text on the teleprompter and the text in his mind were not the same. The operator, not knowing this, finally decided that the trouble must be position. They began rolling the platform up a bit and then down a bit. The general effect, as Church described it later, was a blur of moving words wherever he looked and a grinding of gears as the platform moved. Against these odds, it is a wonder that he performed as well as he did.

Frank Church was thirty-five years old when he delivered his keynote address. As I listened to an excerpt from it on the news following his death, I did not even listen to what he was saying. I was too shaken by how his voice —its timber and coloration—was reminiscent of my own voice today. So much of what I have learned about public speaking, things like cadence and phrasing, well-balanced periodic structure, and precise elocution, I did not learn, as he did, from debate coaches or through the study of immortal texts. I learned these things from him almost by osmosis. I learned at night when he read me bedtime stories. I learned sitting across the dinner table from him, as he regaled us with humorous anecdotes or dramatic tales from history, or simply with some incident that had befallen him during the day.

I am now thirty-five years old. I too enjoy the sound of my own voice. I like to play with words. I like to press ideas as far as they will go. I love to tell stories. One criticism of Frank Church was that he took himself too seriously. In fact, he took words and ideas seriously. I know the difference because I learned it from him.

Senator Church's first major assignment in the Senate came during the long debate over the 1957 Civil Rights Act, a comprehensive if not inclusive piece of legislation designed to guarantee equal treatment for citizens regardless of race or beliefs. The champion of the 1957 Civil Rights Act, the first civil rights law since Reconstruction, was Senate Majority Leader Lyndon Johnson. In part, he was basing his own presidential hopes upon extending his constituency beyond the south. On the other hand, there is probably no single figure in our recent history who contributed more to the cause of social justice than Lyndon Johnson. This legislation was a major breakthrough, one of many that he would sponsor. Johnson deserves the credit not only for its passage, but for its coming to the Senate floor at all.

The success of this legislation depended upon the swing votes of senators such as John Kennedy of Massachusetts. Frank Church was brought on as an assistant floor manager of the bill, with the task of fashioning a compromise that could sway their votes and lead to final passage for the act as a whole. He came up with the addendum that integrated all federal juries for the first time. Not only did this pass, but its presence in the legislation guaranteed final passage of the entire bill. As Bethine Church was leaving the revolving door at the front of the Senate side of the Capitol, John Kennedy caught her arm and said, "Your man pulled it off." It was her husband's first major role in the Senate, and she was tremendously proud. So was he. But beyond a sense of personal accomplishment, Church also enjoyed a few tangible benefits from his labors. He received his first bit of national attention and, far more important, the gratitude of Lyndon Johnson.

As Majority Leader, Johnson was better able than anyone to advance Church's Senate career. The first benefit he bestowed upon the young senator from Idaho was appointment to the Labor Rackets Investigating Committee. In later years, Church would devote a major chapter of his career to investigations of the multinational corporations and of the CIA and FBI. In this, his first investigation, he was only a supporting actor. Yet, the initial indication of what would become Frank Church's most characteristic trait, a sense of outrage against practices—whether in business, labor, or government—he believed to be morally wrong, appeared during the course of the Rackets Committee hearings. When Jimmy Hoffa was brought before the committee, in response to the labor leader's condescending apologetics, Church's response was typical. "We don't need you, Mr. Hoffa," he interrupted sharply, "to come up here and moralize on what's right and wrong."

Before long Church had established a reputation for being a tough but fair questioner in public hearings. In 1959, Johnson responded again by advancing Frank Church, over several senators far ahead of him in seniority, to a much coveted seat on the Senate Foreign Relations Committee. Thus began the fulfillment of a young boy's dream. Twenty years later Frank Church would complete that dream by becoming chairman.

Frank Church's first gambit at trying out the chairman's role was a bit of a disaster. As a young senator, newly appointed to the Foreign Relations Committee, Church was asked one day by Senator Fulbright to preside over a public hearing. He could not have been more delighted. In calling the committee to order, he leaned back in the chairman's high-backed swivel chair, no doubt trying to look confident, and toppled over on his head. Righting himself and the chair, he turned to his colleagues and observed, "The junior senator from Idaho is not accustomed to presiding over this lofty committee."

When I was a boy, if you had asked me what a senator did, I probably would have told you that one of the most important things that a senator did was to fight filibusters. Whenever Strom Thurmond or some other sturdy figure on the right wished to parlay a minority position into a victory through stalemate, he would filibuster. It required two-thirds of the senators to vote cloture, the rule that would force a senator to stop speaking. Accordingly, if you had as many as thirty-four solid votes against a given piece of legislation, you could, at least in theory, hold out forever. Like hell, filibusters seemed almost never to freeze over. Instead they thawed the resolve of the opposition, leading often to a stalemate, which was as good as a victory for those who were eager to obstruct some law, almost always a civil rights law, from being passed.

There was one additional gambit that a filibustering group could employ. As one's opponents—the majority favoring the bill—grew weary of waiting, the troops could secretly be mustered and a roll call asked for. This meant that a sufficient number of senators had to stand guard against this ploy. As the youngest senator and one of the most junior, Frank Church received on such occasions what amounted to permanent guard duty.

For a child all this was very exciting. My father would sleep night after night on a cot in the Democratic cloakroom. We would visit him there. He would not bother to shave. It was as if he were a part of some great and elemental struggle against evil. I spent more hours at the Senate during filibusters than at any other time. I must admit that, while my father never seemed to enjoy them very much, filibusters certainly did add a sense of drama to a young boy's life.

Though they were never to feel completely at home in Washington, Frank and Bethine relished Church's first term in the Senate. His descriptions of that period alter-

nate between awe and joy at being a senator. This is
captured in a letter Frank wrote to Bethine in August of
1961 on one of the rare occasions when the two of them
were apart.

"Last night I went to New York City to Elmo Roper's
dinner. It proved to be a very interesting affair. There
were 12 of us, including Bill Fulbright and Adlai Stevenson, who were Elmo's other two guests of honor. I
thought it was a little curious that all of the wealthy
people Elmo invited indicated that they were coming,
until I learned the identification of the other two guests
of honor. Anyhow, Henry Luce ('my friends call me
"Harry"') of *Time, Life* and *Fortune*, was there along
with Will Clayton, the Texas millionaire; Roger Stevens,
whose wife is so interested in humane treatment of ani-
mals; a Mr. Christie, who owns the iron ore mines in
Liberia, and is said to have been the largest single con-
tributor to Adlai Stevenson's campaign in 1952; a Mr.
Welch, the president of some little enterprise known as
the 'Standard Oil Company'; a Mr. Wellington, a well-
known investment banker of Wall Street; and a Mr.
Wright, who is the editor of *This Week* magazine, which
is circulated in so many of the major Sunday newspapers.

" 'Harry' Luce pulled me aside to say that whatever
treatment I had received in *Time* magazine, he personally felt that my keynote address had been extremely
effective. He said that he regretted it at the time, because
he opposed the Democratic cause, but that he wanted me
to know what his personal reaction had been. This
confirmed what you will remember Kennedy had told us
the day following his nomination in Los Angeles. I told
Luce that for one not interested in the Democratic cause,
his publications had much to do with the tremendous
buildup of Kennedy in the crucial months prior to the
convention. Luce allowed as that was so, but he added,

'When the conventions were over, I was for Nixon, and I put out plenty of banana peels for Kennedy to slip on, but somehow he kept stepping around them, while Nixon did all the slipping.'

"At about this time, Stevenson appeared, and Luce said to me, sourly, 'I thought we were going to have dinner, but we're going to have Adlai instead.'

"After dinner I put forward the subject 'Resolved we should commence a vigorous public debate on the impending Berlin crisis' as the proposition for discussion. It turned out to be a very lively discussion and I nearly missed my plane back to Washington. But when I had to leave, Stevenson left with me, which gave us a chance to have a short private conversation en route to his hotel. He was distressed that he would have to abstain today on the Tunisian resolution relating to Bizerte. He felt that the abstention was wrong, and so do I. It looks like I got my speech in on 'Our New African Policy' just in time —while we still had one! As Adlai left the taxi, he had his little revenge. 'Come back to New York, Frank, when we can spend an evening in conversation together without having to waste half of our time listening to Luce!' "

My Washington years might very well have come to a close in 1962. In the history of Idaho politics a Democrat had never been reelected to the United States Senate. Idaho is a conservative state. In his early years, Frank Church was perhaps more moderate in his politics than he was to become as his philosophy developed. Even then, however, he stood far to the left of the majority of people in Idaho. Furthermore, the harder he tried to convince his constituents of his point of view the clearer it became to them that his politics and theirs were incompatible. As the election drew near, Church began to awaken to the fact that he was in trouble back home.

Frank Church did have one very important thing going for him, however. It is something that would serve him well throughout his political career. While he focused much of his own time and thought on issues relating to foreign policy, he remained mindful of the people who had elected him and joined his staff in attending assiduously to constituent services. Before long it came to be known that if you had a personal problem with your Social Security check or a federal regulatory agency, if your wife died and your son was in the service in Germany, if your business was collapsing and you did not know how to file bankruptcy, the person to call was Frank Church. It is surely an exaggeration, but it was rumored in the state that Church would return a call to one of his constituents before he would return a call to the White House.

Among my mother's letters I found this amusing illustration.

October 4, 1957

Mrs. Frank F. Church
109 West Idaho Street
Boise, Idaho

Dear Mrs. Church:

It has recently been called to my attention that your household has been blessed with the addition of an infant son. May I extend to you my heartiest congratulations and best wishes upon his arrival.

I am happy to be of service to you, and I am enclosing, with my compliments, a book published by the United States Department of Health, Education and Welfare entitled, "INFANT CARE."

If I may be of service to you in the future, I hope you will feel free to call upon me.

Sincerely,

Frank Church
United States Senator

One of the principal reasons that Church was re-elected time and again was that people tend to care most deeply about things that affect their daily lives. Personal concerns outweigh public ones. Local issues are often more important than state issues, and state issues of greater concern than national or international ones. If their senator could be counted upon to help them in those areas that mattered to them most, they could forgive him for an occasional lapse of judgment elsewhere.

Even so, Frank Church's seat was far from safe. In 1962 his opponent was Jack Hawley, a lawyer from Boise. Hawley was from an old and respected Idaho family. He was a moderate Republican. This made him attractive both to conservative Democrats and also to those less ideological members of his own party who might be reluctant to support someone far to their political right. Furthermore, Hawley was bright, young, and rugged-looking. He proved to be a strong competitor and ran a clean if hard campaign. By October the race was too close to call.

One major issue in the campaign was the use of Idaho's wilderness areas. This issue was to grow in moment over the next six years, but Church was already vulnerable in Idaho as one who was antidevelopment. Shortly before the election, his father-in-law, who as well as any man knew how the user groups had historically dominated Idaho politics, said, "Tell me, Frank, how do you expect to win? All the organizations that count are against you: the cattlemen, the woolgrowers, the mining association, the forest products industry, the newspapers [all but one supported Hawley], the chambers of commerce . . . and for what? For wilderness! You don't just have rocks on your mind; you've got rocks in your head!"

Clark had not exhausted the list. The doctors and dentists were also against him, but that was on account of Medicare.

One foreign affairs issue that was simmering beneath the surface in Idaho was Cuba. Church was reputed to be soft on communism. Cuba became a testing ground for his patriotism. In response to this, Church went to Guantánamo and was briefed by the military, following which he put out a detailed newsletter to Idaho saying that, if there were any major threat from that quarter, he, as a member of the Foreign Relations Committee and a personal friend of President Kennedy, would be among the first to know. Church was fully briefed on developments there, he said, and he could report with great confidence that we had nothing to worry about.

The afternoon the newsletter arrived in people's mailboxes in Idaho, Frank Church watched President Kennedy's somber announcement to the country of the presence of Soviet missiles on the island of Cuba. As he and Bethine were driving toward their next campaign stop, Church turned to his wife and said, "The campaign is over." They pulled their car off to the side of the road. It was almost dusk. The sky was already dark. It was pouring rain. "There is one chance," he said. "I have to find a phone."

Right around the corner, there on the banks of the Clearwater River, was a gas station. From a pay phone booth, Church called the White House. Bobby Kennedy came on the line, and Church said to him, "I am embarrassed even to be calling you at a time like this. I will understand fully if there is nothing you can do for me, but just today I assured the people of my state that we have nothing to worry about in Cuba. What can I do?"

The White House could not have been more responsive. Within twelve hours, Church was back in Boise standing on an airfield surrounded by local reporters and awaiting the arrival of an air force plane that had been dispatched to rush him back to Washington for consultations. Church was briefed at the White House upon his arrival. From there, he went directly to the studio and delivered a live television report to the people of Idaho.

Fortunately, Frank Church was chairman of the Foreign Relations Special Committee on International Organizations. Since the debate was taking place on this issue in the United Nations, where Adlai Stevenson was ambassador, Church flew to New York, met regularly with Stevenson, and phoned back to Idaho blow-by-blow accounts of the U.S.-Soviet negotiations, including the compromise over U.S. bases in Turkey. These personal updates were repeated every few hours until the crisis had passed. When Church returned to Idaho, he was met not with anger but with honor. Two weeks later he was reelected to the Senate, defeating Jack Hawley by 25,000 votes.

I spent the 1962 campaign working in the Democratic Party storefront headquarters in Boise. I was fourteen years old. Again, I split my ninth-grade year between Boise and Washington. One of the things I did that year was experiment with changing my name. It was about time to give up Twig, and so for about three months at school I tried Frank on for size. Though ultimately it did not fit, at that point in my life it was very exciting being Frank Church, especially in Idaho. Even then, however, there were periods of confusion and moments of pain.

I spent a great deal of time that year with my old friend Jimmy Bruce. One day we were playing outside his house, and a passerby complained about the way we were behaving. Whatever we had done I do not remember, but this man was very abusive and Jimmy ended up in tears. Jimmy's father, a senior executive at the Idaho Power Company and an old friend of our family, was infuriated, not at us but at the passing stranger. "Listen, mister, you have no right to speak to my son that way," big Jim Bruce shouted. Barely able to contain his anger, he lowered his voice and said, "Jimmy's a damn fine boy. A man who is running for United States senator has told me that Jimmy is the finest boy he knows." "Who is that?" taunted the man. I stood there proudly. Mr. Bruce replied, "Jack Hawley."

Both Jimmy Bruce and his dad were at my father's funeral in Boise. They came over to the Clark house where we all gathered afterward, and we had a wonderful reunion. I expect that 1962 was the only year that Jim Sr. voted against my father. It is also the last time that Jack Hawley did. Hawley was converted by Church's stand on Vietnam. "The most impressive thing about him," Hawley was later to say, "was the real gutsy stand against the war. He was pretty consistent on that. He had the guts to be against it early. I've voted for him ever since."

In early 1965, Frank Church became the fourth U.S. senator to break with the President over Vietnam. Church had begun to doubt the wisdom of American policy in the Far East as early as 1963. Not only did he express his concern to President Kennedy in private, but that same year Church went public with a resolution conditioning further U.S. aid to South Vietnam upon the Diem government's halting its religious persecution of the Buddhist monks. In 1964, Frank Church did support the Gulf of Tonkin resolution, reasoning that the Democrats should stick together to help defeat Barry Goldwater. He regretted that vote to the end of his life. It was not long, however, before he took a stand. On February 5, 1965, speaking on the same day but without design, Frank Church and George McGovern joined Wayne Morse of Oregon and Ernest Gruening of Alaska in expressing opposition to the growing American involvement in Southeast Asia. That morning, Church delivered his first major speech on Vietnam in the Senate chamber. It clearly sounds the themes that Church was to return to time and again throughout the remainder of his political career.

"In the span of thirty years, an excess of isolationism has been transformed into an excess of interventionism. . . . Why? . . . The answer, I think, stems from our intensely ideological view of the cold war. We have come to treat 'communism,' regardless of what form it may take in any given country, as the enemy. We fancy ourselves as the guardian of the 'free' world, though most of it is not free, and never has been. We seek to immunize this world against further Communist infection through massive injections of American aid, and wherever necessary, through direct American intervention. Such a vast undertaking has at least two defects: first, it exceeds our national capability; second, among the newly emerging nations, where the specter of Western imperialism is dreaded more than communism, such a policy can be self-defeating."

Bethine Church vigorously opposed her husband's decision to deliver this speech. Not only were she and Lady Bird Johnson the closest of friends, but she was painfully aware of the potential impact Church's position might have on his political future in Idaho. Church's father-in-law, Chase Clark, was so bewildered by it that, during the final two years of his life, the subject of Vietnam was scrupulously avoided whenever the two of them were together. And, above all others, Lyndon Johnson was furious. More than anyone else he had been responsible for Church's advancement in the Senate. Johnson believed in loyalty. It was one thing for Church to have supported Kennedy in the Democratic presidential primaries in 1960, but now Johnson was President of the United States. As such, when it came to directing the course of American foreign policy, he would brook no insubordination, especially from a member of his own party. Church himself was to say, in response to a question about the political fallout from his stand on Vietnam, "I won't always have to live with my job. But I'll always have to live with my conscience."

Shortly after Church's call for a negotiated settlement to end the war, the pressure began. Senator Church and his wife were invited to the White House for dinner. When the company was assembled, Johnson opened his remarks by saying that sometimes senators thought they knew more about war and peace than the President. He asked them not to forget a certain senator from Idaho, William Borah, who predicted there would be no war in Europe before World War I, and opposed our entry into World War II.

"He had me fixed in a burning gaze," Church was to report later in an interview with Mary Perot Nichols for the *Village Voice*. "He was revved up like a carnival barker." When drinks were served, as Church recalled, President Johnson "came through the crowd like a dreadnought toward me." Standing up to demonstrate how LBJ got people "at a psychological disadvantage," Church said, "he turned his head down until we were kind of nostril to nostril." Was he scared? "No," said Church without a moment's hesitation. "I kept wondering how I was going to get a word in . . . I got my punches in where I could. I remember that Gene McCarthy said later that if I had just surrendered, everybody could have left thirty minutes earlier."

At one point in the conversation, Church cited his agreement with Walter Lippmann on one particular point. "Later I realized LBJ wished he had said to me what he had not said," Church continued. "So the next day he told the press he had said it anyway. He said that he had told me, 'The next time you want a dam in Idaho, you go to Walter Lippmann for it.'"

A few weeks later, President Johnson delivered a speech at Johns Hopkins in which he introduced the concept of "unconditional negotiations." Before this he had refused to admit the possibility of any form of negotiations with regard to Vietnam. Before the speech, Johnson called Church and George McGovern to the White House to preview the text. "McGeorge Bundy showed us the speech," Church said, "and then LBJ granted us an audience. Jack Valenti was there also." Church described Johnson sitting behind a big desk like a bust of Napoleon III. " 'Frank, how's the dam building going out in Idaho?' he asked. 'Just fine,' I replied. 'The next dam we get will be called the Walter Lippmann Dam.' " Church described Bundy's and Valenti's faces blanching. "Then Johnson laughed," said Church, pausing for effect, "and *then* they laughed. LBJ said, 'I wonder who got that story started.' 'I don't know,' " said Church. To which Johnson, closing the discussion, said, "Oh, probably some Republican."

My father was agonizing over Vietnam long before I was. The war would soon divide us, however, even as it did so many other children and their parents during the late 1960s. Several of my high school classmates were to die in Vietnam. But in 1965, both death and war were unimaginable to us as we cheered the incongruously named Walt Whitman Vikings on to victory and huddled in packs at the sock hops and cruised the streets of Bethesda. Then my interests were focused more upon the Beatles, girls, and student politics than they were upon international affairs. That spring, I ran for senior class president and lost. I began my speech, "As the cow said to the farmer on a cold winter's morning, thanks for the warm hand." It was all downhill from there.

Walt Whitman was filled with exceptional students. Fifty in my senior class alone were National Merit scholars. I was not among them. One of them licked his fingers in a home LSD lab and has been in and out of mental institutions ever since. One dropped out of college and joined a religious cult. Many of us over the next four years were to flirt with or be wooed by self-destruction. It almost seems as if too much consciousness at an early age was the curse of my generation.

At first, I was spared this. I carried little weight on my shoulders. Life seemed nothing more than a lark. In a way, I was still a child of the fifties. My closest friends and I did not even discover beer until the final semester of our senior year. We were self-absorbed, but in a conventional way. I did well enough in school, but hardly stood out. My parents were unperturbed. I cannot remember ever being asked if I had done my homework. Often I had not. I graduated 116th in a class of 600. My College Board scores were good enough, however, to ensure early acceptance to Stanford University. And so in 1966, I left home for school in California, still following my father's footsteps.

3. San Francisco

key story!

During the middle of my sophomore year at Stanford, my closest college friend died of pneumonia while on a skiing vacation at Vail, Colorado. He had been out on the slopes just the day before. That morning he felt a little tired and somewhat congested, so he stayed in the cabin while his friends skied. When they returned home later in the afternoon, he was dead.

Dalton Denton was blithe of spirit, serious about things but not at all somber. He was tremendously good fun to be with, and we spent almost all our free time together. He introduced me to Scotch and Beethoven, two habits he had picked up at Exeter. I suppose that he was the closest thing to a sophisticate that I had ever encountered. We were dorm mates in our freshman year. Together we pursued two striking girls, both actresses, who were themselves best friends. And, more than once, after an all-night conversation Dalton and I saw in the dawn.

At the beginning of our sophomore year, Dalton, five other friends of ours, and I moved into the Theta Xi fraternity house. The previous spring we had rushed as

64

a group. The rules we set up for ourselves were clearly stated from the outset. If any one of us was not acceptable, none of us would accept the fraternity's bid. To ensure the success of this enterprise we chose the weakest fraternity on campus.

Later I learned that my father had lived at Theta Xi after the war. It was no stronger then. He told me about his years at the fraternity only after I had joined. The full picture of how remarkably similar our fraternity experiences were came clear to me only after my father's death while reading his letters.

When we discussed this some years ago, my father couldn't remember if he had actually been inducted into the secrets or not. He had. He was something like Tau 305. Tau was our chapter. Each of our numbers was put on a star in the secret meeting chamber. If I remember correctly, I was Tau 619. I expect that our stars are burning there still against the cobalt blue walls. As I discovered when he came to visit me that fall, my father and I even lived in the same room, the best room in the house. I rated this honor by being chosen by the president of our house as his roommate. How my father was so fortunate I never thought to ask. In one of his letters to Bethine he writes, "Dave Bluford and I share a comfortable room up on the third deck of the Theta Xi house, a room made especially attractive by the fact that Dave owns a sizable library, housed in three separate bookcases, some fifty albums of records, an excellent Victrola, a radio, a cabinet, a large lamp, and one of the easiest of easy chairs. All of this leaves just enough room for my scanty property, and provides us with an exceedingly cozy, academic-appearing refuge." As far as I can remember of my own brief stay there, in twenty years the room had hardly changed at all.

I scorned the fraternity system almost as much as others in the system scorned Theta Xi. The plan that my friends and I concocted was simple. We would move in and quickly take over the house. The price was right, and being located on campus, it would serve as a convenient commune. The seven of us did constitute a majority of the fall pledge class that year at Theta Xi; however, taking over was not as simple a matter as I imagined it would be.

One night, after a particularly raucous party, we pledges were awakened from our beds and lined up downstairs in our underwear. I had not even considered the possibility, but we were about to be hazed. The initial act of obedience that was required of us was the first of many I refused to perform. It was three o'clock in the morning and I was not about to put a piece of liver down my shorts. As I look back on it, the two most surprising things about the following twenty-four hours were, first, that no one forced me to do anything, and second, that all of my friends were perfectly happy to go along with whatever games they were told to play.

In my father's letters to my mother I discover this from February of 1947: "This is 'Hell' week on the farm, the time when fraternity pledges get initiated. I may have told you of my displeasure with fraternities. Some of the practices that are now being flaunted are unbelievable. I've managed a working arrangement in the house that leaves me unmolested, but Carl [Burke] has caused a great furor down at Kappa Sig that has been rather bitter at the edges. It seems that every time he misses a function, he gets fined, and he makes a point of missing all the functions. Since he has no money to pay the fines, consternation over the whole affair reigns at Kappa Sig."

As for me, at the end of what has to have been the mildest hazing session in fraternity history, my friends and I were taught the secret handshake and inducted into the brotherhood. Two weeks later, having found an

66

apartment underneath a house nestled in the foothills above Stanford, I left Theta Xi.

Dalton was hurt and angry when I left. He accused me of petulance and unwarranted pride. I accused him of succumbing to a foolish, childish set of rules and rites. For almost two months we did not speak to one another. During this same period I almost left Stanford. I went home to Idaho during Thanksgiving break. My courses were not going well. My father prevailed upon me to return to school and at least finish the year. I dropped one course and salvaged the three others. Nevertheless, I was very much alone, estranged from my friends, and wholly without bearings or a sense of direction.

A week before Dalton died, the two of us spent an entire day together. We drove back and forth along the highway between Stanford and the sea. And we talked. We talked about the search. We talked about death. I told him that I did not expect to live past the age of twenty-five. From my perspective today, it was almost as if I assumed that I would die in place of my father. At the time, it was simply a dark, romantic notion. It was part of a desperate attempt to feel life deeply, this at a time when I was struggling to feel anything at all.

Dalton was sympathetic, but unimpressed. He told me that both of us had so very much to live for. Our lives were just beginning. There was no reason for us to view everything and every day in ultimate terms. It was enough to live and love as best we could. Dalton too was a romantic, but of the starry kind. He was at peace with himself and at home in the world. Despite my happy childhood, for some reason, at this juncture in my life, I was not. Mine was a classic case of rebellion, done by the numbers.

Dalton told me two things that I have repeated many times over the years. "Accept yourself, Forrest, and you will be able to forgive others," he said. And then he

quoted St. Augustine, "Love, and do what you will."
What a blessing that day was, for both of us, I think.
It resulted in a total reconciliation between us. And his
love that day was not the final gift Dalton Denton gave
to me. That gift came in self-renewing and ever increasing installments after he died. It is the gift of memory.
I had lost someone I loved. Each time I remembered him,
our last day together, the twinkle in his eye, I was reminded of how fragile life is, and how precious.

Now, years later, I find myself touching on this theme
Sunday after Sunday. The past is over. Besides, if we
pine over it, what we are pining for is probably much
different in selective memory than it was in reality. As
for the future, we can do so little about it. Longing for
something in the future only takes time away from our
embracing the present. Wishful thinking is sloppy and
sentimental. How much better it would be if we indulged in a bit more "thoughtful wishing," thinking to
wish for what is ours this very day, ours to savor and to
save.

Dalton's death was a major turning point in my life.
I had been playing games with myself and others, rely-
ing upon my own pathos to create a personal context for
meaning. Death was far more real than I had imagined
it to be. I began then in earnest to piece together my
religion. If religion is our human response to the dual
reality of being alive and having to die, I had experienced
my first real encounter with the life and death questions
to which with increasing energy I would devote the remainder of my life.

This was not the most important thing that happened
to me during my college years, however. The following
fall, I met the woman who was to become my wife. I met
Amy Furth at Branner Hall, a coed freshman dormitory
at which I had chosen, for strategic reasons, to eat my
meals when on campus. Amy was an incoming fresh-

man. She was a native of the San Francisco Bay area, a fourth-generation Californian. I was taken by her instantly, and by the beginning of October had succeeded in prevailing upon her to go out on a date with me.

Our first date might easily have been our last. I asked Amy out for dinner. We were going to double-date with two of my more impressive friends. This fell through, but I had a backup plan that she did not know about. In a classic bait and switch, when I picked her up—wearing the uniform of the day, a workshirt and jeans—I told her that while dinner had not worked out I had a splendid alternative. We were going to the beach.

It was a warm October night. She was overdressed for the occasion, but I had brought a blanket along and a bottle of wine. Everything in fact would have turned out fine if, on leaving the beach, we had not run into a merry company of Chicanos. We joined them for another cup of wine. We were having a perfectly pleasant time, when all of a sudden one of them began to test me. The question was this: Was I man enough to steal my date a pumpkin?

I had never stolen anything in my life, and Amy was absolutely opposed to the idea, but I rose to his bait. There were fields and fields of pumpkins all along the side of the road between the beach and the foothills. They were there for the taking. If I had any kind of pluck whatsoever I would "get one for the little lady." And so I did. We drove down the dark highway. There was not a soul to be seen for miles. It was midnight and pitch black outside. I stopped at the side of the road, walked out into the field, and picked two tremendous pumpkins. By the time I returned to the car, the police had arrived.

It was October 1968. My father was up for reelection to the Senate in three short weeks. Amy and I sat in the back of the police car. There were six empty beer cans and a gun on the floor. He started to ask me questions, routine questions, like what my father did for a living. I said that he worked for the U.S. government. "What level?" he asked. "GS 13, GS 14?"

"Oh," I replied, "about GS 20, I think." I was mortified. The last thing my father needed was to receive a call from the police informing him that his son had been arrested stealing pumpkins in California.

Fortunately, the patrolman had a different agenda. He drove us to a farmhouse just a short distance away. Out came a farmer wearing a long white nightshirt and a tasseled nightcap. "I understand you are interested in purchasing a couple of pumpkins," he said.

"Yes, sir," I replied. "I would very much like to purchase a couple of pumpkins."

"Do you have any particular pumpkins in mind?"

"These two would be fine," I said.

"That will be fifteen dollars, son." Never has so little blood money purchased a sweeter release. I was free from the law, Amy went out with me again, and my father was reelected to the United States Senate.

Frank Church was the first United States senator to be targeted for defeat by national extremist groups such as the John Birch Society on account of his dovish stance on Vietnam. He seemed an easy mark. Idaho was a small, conservative state. A relatively modest amount of money would go a long way there, both for the purchase of paid media and for blanket mailings. The same principle obtained in 1980 when NCPAC, the most extreme and best financed of several right-wing political action committees, poured more money into Idaho than into any other state in their national effort to unseat liberal senators. In the mid-1960s, however, this tactic was untried and the methods chosen much less sophisticated than would be the case twelve years later. While one such group did play a major, if bizarre, role in Church's 1968 campaign for reelection, this proved far more a boon than a blow to Church's hopes.

In 1967, a wealthy member of the John Birch Society, a cosmetics manufacturer from southern California, bankrolled a recall campaign against Church on the grounds of treason. His agent was a dogcatcher from the tiny town of St. Maries, Idaho. This effort backfired in two important ways. First, Church was drawn fully into his own fight for reelection far earlier than he might otherwise have been. Second, the people of Idaho, regardless of their politics, took umbrage at the notion of an outsider trying to dictate their own electoral destiny. Add to this the wholly untempered language that was employed—in the recall literature Church was called a "Commie-symp" who had been kept in office by "Pinkos" and "Punks"—and all the makings for a backlash were in place. After a two-month effort only 159 signatures had been gathered on the recall petitions. It would have died on its own merit, but the courts ruled that the effort was illegal. As a final poetic twist, a few years later the right-wing dogcatcher, having decided that he had been manipulated by outsiders, announced that he would support Church in his next election.

Even lacking this misbegotten escapade, Church probably would have survived the 1968 election. The people of Idaho may not have agreed with Church's position on Vietnam, but neither did they care much for Lyndon Johnson. As Church was to reflect several years later, "The fact that I was a Democrat who opposed him established my independence, and even though people disagreed with my opposition to the war, they were madder at Johnson than they were at my dissent."

In addition to Vietnam, Church was vulnerable on several other counts. His opponent, Second District Congressman George Hansen, hammered away at Church's civil rights and antipoverty legislation, and also at his support of the nuclear test ban treaty. None of these issues packed as much emotional wallop, however, as did Church's increasingly vigorous championship of environmental causes.

Church had not always been a strong conservationist. In 1957 he advocated the building of a seven-hundred-foot-high dam in the Hell's Canyon, the deepest gorge in North America, in order to generate power for mining the phosphate fields of southeastern Idaho. "I believe we have a trust," he said then, "not only to ourselves but to our children, to develop the full potential of our God-given resources." Fourteen years later, in a complete about-face, Church was to wage an unsuccessful battle against the Idaho Power Company to preserve this same canyon. Finally, he would succeed in designating the last undammed stretch on the Snake River as a national recreation area. In between, he had shifted from being a senator friendly to the developers to one of the most outspoken environmentalists in Congress.

In his second term in the Senate, as a member of the Senate Interior Committee, Frank Church authored or helped draft the two cornerstones of wild lands preservation. In 1964, he was a coauthor, sponsor, and floor leader for the Wilderness Act, which set aside undeveloped federal lands to be "untrammeled by man; where man is a visitor who does not remain." In 1968, Church authored and led the floor fight for the Wild and Scenic Rivers Act, an equally extensive piece of legislation, which preserved certain stretches of America's most spectacular rivers in their natural, free-flowing state. Both bills were hotly contested in Congress, but they finally won passage. Later Senator George McGovern was to credit Church with being "an extraordinarily able floor manager. He did it by shaming people into standing for the future of this country—despite all the special interest claims."

Church accomplished this at no little cost to himself

and his family. I have mentioned the sale in 1972 of Robinson Bar Ranch, the Clark family homestead where Frank and Bethine were married in 1947 and where I summered as a boy. But throughout his Senate career, the repercussions in Idaho of Church's ever more aggressive support of wilderness legislation were considerable, involving him in more than one pitched battle for political survival. In 1983, three years following his defeat for reelection to the Senate, Church reminisced in a speech to Idaho conservationists, admitting that he welcomed certain things about being out of public life.

"There are, I might say, some advantages to being sidelined. No longer must I preside at crowded public hearings, as in Grangeville, while being hung in effigy outside; or abide the taunts of angry witnesses who'd been led to believe, mistakenly, that their jobs in the woods and lumber mills were being threatened. During those frays, I marveled at how my wife, Bethine, managed to keep her cool. On one occasion, the public hearing in Salmon on my bill to authorize the River of No Return Wilderness, a cowboy flaunted his contempt by riding his horse through the front entrance of the hall, down the center aisle, out the side door. The wide-eyed editor of the local paper turned to Bethine and blurted out, 'Well, what did you think of that?' 'Why,' she replied, 'I thought that was a right handsome horse.'"

The 2.2-million-acre River of No Return Wilderness, the largest protected wilderness area in the continental United States, was renamed the Frank Church–River of No Return Wilderness Area the month before he died. When Senator William Proxmire noted a certain inappropriateness in the name, Senator Dale Bumpers replied that, under whatever name, there could be no more appropriate memorial to a man who had given so much energy to the protection of our natural heritage.

Frank Church's opponent in 1968 has since become

famous in his own right, although he did not become notorious until years after his defeat for the Senate. At the time, George Hansen was a charismatic young congressman, an eloquent champion of conservative causes. On one occasion during the 1968 campaign, Congressman Hansen's wife, Connie, apologized to my mother during an encounter following a parade for riding in a pink saddle suit. "It's really out of character," she said. "Just imagine! How could they ever have given *me* a pink saddle suit!"

Hansen was a tireless campaigner. At six feet six, he towered over the crowds. He proved unequal to Church in a series of debates, but in many other ways George Hansen was a formidable opponent. The breaks went against him, however, and despite the fact that Richard Nixon swept Idaho by the largest margin of any presidential candidate in history, Hansen lost to Church by an even larger margin than Nixon's. In what would turn out to be Church's strongest victory, he defeated George Hansen by 173,482 to 114,394 votes. A joke went around Idaho following Church's victory. "I don't understand how he won. I've never met anyone who admitted voting for him." Two years later Hansen returned to Congress. Since then he has emerged off and on in the national spotlight, but almost always featured in court as a defendant charged with violations of the House Ethics Code and Campaign Finance Law.

Twenty years old and halfway through my college career, I was worse than useless to my father during the 1968 campaign. I did agree to stay in Idaho, but would not campaign. I pulled chain at a lumber mill that summer. The rest of the time, I lived in the basement of the Clark family house on Idaho Street in Boise. It was more of a boiler room than a basement, but I turned it into a romantic grotto, a kind of good-guys hideout from the outside world. I painted the pipes black and silver and gold. I brought down my record player, my books, and my typewriter. Later I discovered that my father's chief advisers referred to me as a ticking time bomb, George Hansen's secret weapon. Sometimes one starts to grow up at the wrong time. For instance, my entire library was made up of Russian novels and books about the Russian Revolution. For the first time in my life, I was completely engrossed in something outside of myself. The thing I was engrossed in, however, could not have been more inopportune for my father.

My father and I were almost completely estranged during this period. I can remember trying to talk to him. It was almost hopeless. One of the reasons was that my passions were so high and my experience and knowledge so thin. I had stopped wearing a watch. I had stopped reading the newspaper. Everything that he had devoted his life to struck me as superficial, and yet, when we talked, his advantage over me was great. He was thinking and I was feeling. This led to enormous frustration on both of our parts. When I could not explain what I felt, when he tripped up my arguments with logic, I was wounded and angry. Regardless of the subject, I had this deep feeling that I was right. His counterpoint seemed like callous and jesuitical reasoning to me. I can remember how furious I was when we would have a discussion and I could not express clearly what I wished to say. Once I even burst into tears. I hated myself for this, for my inability to present adequately in words the truth I so deeply felt; and I hated my father for exposing this weakness by his quiet, if impatient, questioning. Ultimately, the only response left to me was simply to retreat into a vale of self-righteousness.

Much of the burden of these discussions stemmed from my declaration of pacifism. Despite their opposition to the Vietnam war, my parents could not understand this. I, in turn, could not understand how they could fail at least to recognize the legitimacy of my own position. Much of our estrangement, however, had nothing to do with issues. It had to do with my own emergent and inarticulate discovery of self, this at a time when my parents were fighting for political survival.

I had come to hate politics. I was desperately looking for something to believe in. Despite the trouble I had in expressing myself, there were no shadings in my thought between good and evil or truth and falsehood. As far as I could see it, everything my parents were involved in, belabored as it was with inevitable compromise, was a sham. My parents and I were getting nowhere in our attempts to work things out together. Carl Burke tried to intervene, but without success. Fortunately, summer was almost over. My return to Stanford in the fall was a relief to everyone concerned.

It is hard to pinpoint when one begins to grow up. I suppose, more than anything else, it has to do with the shouldering of responsibility. If this is so, I finally began to come of age when I turned twenty-one. At twenty-one years old, I was graduated from college and got married. At the time, the latter of these two passages may not have seemed like a responsible act. When Amy told her parents that we wanted to get married, they quickly submitted a counteroffer, a year in Italy with a side trip to Russia. Admittedly, I had no prospects. What they failed to understand was that prospects were passé.

It was the spring of 1970. My last quarter of college had been spent manning the barricades. Protesting the invasion of Cambodia, my classmates and I had shut Stanford University down. As far as we were concerned, with this action and those like it across the country things had been changed forever. There would never again be anything remotely resembling life as usual. The future we might once have anticipated was suspended, because the past could no longer be counted on as a guide for us.

Reason was in shambles, because manifestly reasonable people had mired us in an insane war. Everything our parents stood for was thus exposed in our eyes as a fraud. That my father at this very juncture in our history was writing the legislation that would finally put a stop to the invasion of Cambodia, that he and a handful of others in the U.S. Senate had struggled for years within the system to bring the Vietnam war to a close, made little difference to me then. The system he was fighting to preserve from its own folly was finished, or so we passionately believed.

The year we got married, Amy was a sophomore at Stanford. We had lived together since September in a commune of sorts, complete with a dog, two cats, and a goat. My father visited us in November when on a speaking tour in northern California. He was never one to pry into my private life, but his pleasure at my having found a young woman so manifestly superior to those I had brought home in the past seemed to encourage a more supportive response than I might have expected. His primary concern was that I would lose her.

Amy's parents, quite understandably, were less pleased. I wore pants that were held together at the crotch with a safety pin. I wrote poetry on an electric typewriter and left the droppings from my three-hole punch all over the rug whenever I visited their home. Furthermore, their daughter was only nineteen years of age and marriage to anyone at that particular juncture seemed not only a risk but also a terrible waste. Years later, when Amy received her master's at Harvard and became dean of students at the Harvard Divinity School, we could boast to ourselves that the risk had been worthwhile, but they knew the odds far better than we, and were surely justified in their doubts. Fortunately, however, once their headstrong daughter had confirmed her intention to marry me, they supported us fully. We were married in their garden on May 30, 1970, a day that Amy's grandmother, based upon a lifetime of experience, prophetically predicted rain-free.

Of course, we wrote our own ceremony. As a minister who has now performed almost five hundred weddings, I still inwardly flinch when a couple tell me that they are planning to do the same. It brings back so many mixed and powerful memories. Amy's and my vows were not really vows. They were more in the order of a manifesto. And yet as I look back on them, I am in awe at their clarity. It leads me to hope that over the years we have not lost too much of the vision and purpose that inspired us on that day.

My father almost did not make the ceremony. The Cooper-Church Amendment, designed to put a cap on our growing involvement in Southeast Asia, was being debated on the floor of the Senate, and he barely broke free in time to make the last plane west. When my parents arrived I proudly showed them our vows. My mother was audibly appalled. My father just got a little quieter than usual. It was not until years later that I realized how often and how fully they had both bent over backward to avoid getting in my way. They must have been especially conscious of how their position could complicate my life. I, on the other hand, was all but oblivious to how my positions or actions might complicate theirs.

Once, in 1968, someone had hired a band of disreputable-looking longhairs to canvass door to door in northern Idaho, asking people to vote for Frank Church and saying that they were members of my "Hippie Club" in San Francisco. All my father did was, through an intermediary, to ask me to cut my hair and beard. I found the request a painful abridgment of my freedom but reluctantly complied. On this later occasion he simply said, "Forrest, I am not going to tell you what you can or cannot say in your vows to Amy. Your pronouncement of pacifism, however, could not be more poorly timed. All I ask is that you do not release it to the press."

Reluctantly, Amy and I did not distribute the handsomely printed commemorative copy of our vows to the guests. This did not keep the gist of what we had to say from being reported. Among other places it turned up in the Idaho papers and also in the armed forces magazine, the *Stars and Stripes*.

Here is what Amy and I said when we married one another on May 30, 1970:

> *We are joining together in love*
> *in a world of turmoil torn by violence.*
> *We realize that our love will have*
> *little effect upon this world.*
> *It is to each other then,*
> *before our family and friends,*
> *that we wish to pledge our special vows*
> *to guide us and give us strength,*
> *both in our life together,*
> *and when we might be separated.*
>
> *I promise to you, Forrest, to try always*
> *to meet all people without violence;*
> *to respect the life of every person*
> *as a wondrous thing;*
> *to accept injury without bitterness;*
> *and, strengthened by my love for you,*
> *to give only love to others.*
>
> *And, Amy, to you I promise*
> *never to bear arms,*
> *nor to serve in the military.*
> *I promise to try always*
> *to meet all people without violence,*
> *and to share your wonder of life.*

I will try not to resist evil with evil,
and to have compassion
for those who would injure us,
strengthened by my love for you.

We recognize that parenthood is
the greatest responsibility that
two people can share.
Many very sensitive and concerned persons
feel that to bring new life into an
already overburdened world is irresponsibility.
But we feel strongly that our family
will be central to a fulfilling life together.
Whether our children be born
to us or to others,
it is with them in mind
that we make these promises today.

I promise to you, Forrest, that I will try
to be a good mother to our children.
I hope to guide them by the loving example
of my own parents and grandparents,
who have been my guides.

And I promise to you, Amy, that I will try
to be a good father to our children.
I will support you, as I know
you will support me, in their upbringing.
I, too, will remember the example
of loving parents and grandparents.

In some ways, the writing of these words marked the beginning of my reconciliation with my parents. Amy and I had gone further in our declaration of pacifism than they were comfortable with, but a chord of continuity was struck, the example of loving parents and grandparents.

I still felt like an outsider. I admired my father, but felt that my own generation had discovered something much finer, a love that was not particular but universal. We knew enough to recognize that we had not been the first to discover this. St. Francis, Tolstoy, Gandhi, and Martin Luther King, Jr., were our heroes. But we felt, I think, that we were the first *generation* to discover the redemptive power of love. However ill-grounded, this was a powerful feeling, which, ironically, led many of us to repudiate not only our parents but their love for us as well. We were so caught up in our own discovery of love that theirs seemed a cheap imitation, riddled with compromise and unworthy of us.

It was Amy who suggested that we frame these vows in terms of our parents' example. She wrote the words that both of us spoke about parenthood, awakening me to the family bonds that I, a budding existentialist, brave and free, had forgotten to honor. The significance of this did not sink in at once, but it developed surely and steadily over time.

Today, fourteen years later, I read these vows again and am stunned by how suggestive they are of my present aspirations, both as a father and as a minister. The difference is one of experience. I would not change a word, but the words mean more to me now, not only the words about parenting, but also the pledge of nonviolence. Our parents mean more to us, now that we too have children. And, though Amy and I are even more wary than we were then of any pretension that some act of ours could really change the world, we remain fully committed to the principles of nonviolence, viewing them as our only real hope for survival.

If I had only known as we wrote our wedding vows how close my father's own feelings when he was twenty-one had been to my own. In September of 1945, he wrote these prophetic words from China. "There are few endeavors more worthy than that of preventing war. I felt, until a month ago—yet hardly believed, that the common need for peace might avert the sudden outbreak of new war for many years ahead. I knew there could be no lasting peace because nations, jealously guarding their sovereignty, each in pursuit of its own ends, were subservient to no higher authority than their own. There could be no lasting peace because our system of living made war profitable for the few most influential, made war at times essential either to the attainment or to the preservation of wealth and dominance. Finally, primarily, I knew there could be no lasting peace because all peoples were steeped in ideology, the facade for greed, ignorance, prejudice, for distrust, and bigotry, and violent hate. We offered ourselves as bewildered victims in each succeeding massacre.

"But the question of war and peace, I now believe, is locked away in the era that marked our youth. The issue is now a very different one, a challenge as simple as it is inescapable, the kind that all must understand. We have left just two choices, life or death. For the love of God let's have the common sense to accept the undeniable!

"With few exceptions indeed, people I meet over here speak elatedly of the atomic bomb. There are those who tell me, with an expression of the most revealing astonishment, and with incredulous enthusiasm, that our discovery is as yet so imperfect that only one-tenth of one per cent of its total explosive energy has thus far been realized. Apparently it is not enough to have at last developed the instrument of our self-destruction. We even applaud approaching doom! And in a way, Bethy, it is fitting retribution. What could be a more proper finale? For centuries we have synthesized the elements to advance the cause of death. Now we can disintegrate the elements and thus approach the infinite. Let us get on with our work. For it is not surprising that mortal civilization should ultimately confirm the triumph of man's

San Francisco

intellect, the annihilation of man's soul."

Since then we have witnessed staggering advancements in human knowledge and technology. Today we hold in our own hands the powers once assigned to God alone. God's domain, from Genesis to Revelation, from the creation to the apocalypse, has become our own.

This leads to many ironies. I think back on that day during the summer before Amy and I were married, when Neil Armstrong, an American earthling, walked on the moon. The Islamic peoples were scandalized. To them the moon had been desecrated. There would be hell to pay. I was employed in a groundskeeping crew for the Park Service, in Washington, D. C., that summer. My co-workers were offended for a different reason. They did not believe the moonwalk had happened. A Hollywood production, they said, designed to take people's minds off real and pressing problems—the plight of the poor, the racial situation—our own modern equivalent of Marx's characterization of religion as the opiate of the masses.

I remember the astronauts' reading of Genesis 1, broadcast back to earth from the spacecraft on its return flight from the heavens. In Genesis 1 we are said to be formed in the image and likeness of God. "Then God said, 'Let us make humankind in our image, after our likeness; and let them have dominion over the fish of the sea, and over the birds of the air, and over the cattle, and over all the earth. . . . So God created humankind in God's own image . . . male and female he created them. And God blessed them, and said to them, 'Be fruitful and multiply, and fill the earth and subdue it.' " Such dominion gives a haunting turn to one of the phrases with which the moving force behind our space program, John Fitzgerald Kennedy, inaugurated his own New Frontier: "Here on earth," he said, "God's work must truly be our own."

83

In some ways, Amy's and my life together entails a constant renewal of the vows we made to one another that Memorial Day some fourteen years ago, even though the shape our life would take was far from certain then. Like so many of our friends, we were not ready to commit ourselves to a clear future path, perhaps because to do so would entail the sacrifice of a certain degree of our cherished freedom. It would be years before we would discover that without responsibility freedom is an empty shell.

Amy was still a sophomore in college. One of our plans, therefore, was for me to go to graduate school, while Amy finished her degree. I had no idea what I wanted to do or be. I applied to law school at Stanford and divinity school at the Pacific School of Religion in Berkeley. At the same time, Amy and I together put in a bid for a slot in the Peace Corps.

I was accepted by all three. The Stanford option was both the most familiar and the most forbidding. It meant continuing to follow in my father's footsteps. I was spared from having to make a final decision by the terms of their acceptance letter. Stanford was experimenting with a program that would allow and even encourage certain students to get one or two years' life experience before starting law school. This meant that I could go into the Peace Corps, for instance, without jeopardizing my place in some later year's entering class at the law school.

Divinity school was a more distant option. Wayne Rood, the minister who officiated at our wedding, taught at the Pacific School of Religion, but had been at Stanford as interim dean of the chapel during my senior year. After several long discussions, he suggested that I apply to PSR. I had only recently become serious in my schoolwork, and the combination of things that I was most interested in—philosophy, history, and literature—

could easily be pursued at a divinity school. Besides, I suppose I have always been a preacher. In my freshman dorm, even my friends called me "moral man," due, as I remember, to my readiness to interfere with the way that they were living their lives. On the other hand, I did not really know what a minister did, or whether I wanted to become one.

The third option was the Peace Corps. It turned out to be the most appealing. Jerry Brady, the man who had run interference between my father and me during the summer of 1968, was assistant to the director. He helped to secure for us a romantic assignment. Amy and I were to be the entire Peace Corps contingent on a tiny Caribbean island called Bequia. Our job would be to teach English in a little school there. Following our honeymoon at Henry and Charlotte Kimelman's home in the Virgin Islands, we arrived back in the States just in time to set off for six weeks' Peace Corps training just outside Philadelphia. Two days before we were scheduled to begin, President Nixon signed an order mandating that all male Peace Corps candidates agree that, in exchange for a two-year draft deferment, upon completing their tours of duty they would automatically be considered for induction into the army.

Shortly before we got married, I had submitted to my local draft board the forms for conscientious objector status. My father wrote a letter on my behalf. At the time I agreed that, if I could help it, I would do nothing that would precipitate a hearing, which in turn would bring my position to public notice. This was not a purely thoughtful gesture on my part. I had no interest in serving a prison sentence, and it was far from likely that my application would be approved.

In good conscience I could not sign the Peace Corps release form. With my draft number being quite low, that left us with only one real option. We traveled back to California and rented a little apartment on La Conte Avenue in Berkeley, where we began our married life together. Amy transferred to the University of California, and I enrolled in the Master of Divinity program at the Pacific School of Religion. There were positive reasons to take this route: my growing interest in philosophy, ethics, and religion and my new-found desire for a classical education. But the main reason that I went to PSR in the fall of 1970 was to avoid the draft.

Meanwhile, Frank Church continued his work in the Senate. In addition to the Cooper-Church Amendment, barring future involvement by U.S. ground troops in Cambodia, unless specifically authorized by Congress, he later coauthored and gained passage of the Case-Church Amendment, forcing an end to the bombing of Cambodia.

At the same time, Church and Senator Mathias of Maryland were seeking ways to help prevent future Vietnams. For the first time in the history of Congress, a completely bipartisan committee, the Special Committee on Presidential Emergency Powers, was formed with Church, a Democrat, and Mathias, a Republican, as co-chairs. Chairmanships are the prerogative of the side in control of the Senate, but the nature of this committee's work was so unusual that a change was made to account for this. After a lengthy study, Church and Mathias drafted the Emergency Powers Act, which was finally passed and signed into law by President Ford.

To give but one example of the kinds of laws that were being exhumed by the administration to bypass Congress during the Vietnam period, the war effort was often financed without congressional approval through the old cavalry Feed and Forage Act. This act, which had never been struck from the books, enabled our cavalry out west to feed the men and horses without direct instructions from Congress. This made sense because the lines of communication were so poor. Both men and horses might starve before authorization was granted for the purchase of additional supplies.

At first the task of identifying all the extant emergency powers seemed almost impossible. Fortunately, however, the air force, in an attempt to expend all of its appropriated money one year, computerized the entire U.S. Government Code. By punching in key words, it was possible for the Senate committee to assemble a list of all emergency powers from the period of the Civil War forward.

In the past, the problem was that presidents had declared states of emergency, which then had never been removed from the books. In 1972, the United States was operating under as many as 420 states of emergency, some of them going back almost a century. If ever taken out of mothballs and invoked, these offered the President almost unlimited power under law should he choose to exercise it. All previous states of emergency were rescinded by Church and Mathias's legislation, and future states of emergency guaranteed to elapse unless Congress took specific action to extend them. To his credit, President Gerald Ford signed this legislation. To veil it as much as possible from public notice, however, the signing ceremony took place in private. The press was not invited. Only three people were present in the Oval Office: Ford, Mathias, and Church.

During my six years in the San Francisco Bay area, Frank Church emerged from relative obscurity. His relentless struggle against the war in Southeast Asia had gained him national attention, and finally was beginning to bear fruit. What once had been an almost hopeless minority position was no longer. Church had been asked to run for President by the group that eventually turned to Eugene McCarthy to challenge Lyndon Johnson in 1968. Because of his own race for reelection he turned them down. Now, in 1972, George McGovern, Church's closest soul mate in the Senate, was the Democratic presidential nominee.

It was not in the cards that two like-minded Democrats from tiny western states would run together on the same ticket. Senator McGovern did consider Church for the vice-presidential slot, however. In his autobiography, *Grassroots*, McGovern writes somewhat wistfully that, if he had followed his instincts and chosen Church, the principal debacle in his campaign could have been avoided. Later, after Senator Eagleton was asked to withdraw, Church was approached by McGovern, but demurred, arguing that he offered none of the things McGovern so desperately needed by that time in a running mate.

I talked to my father on the phone after this conversation with McGovern. "What did you say to him?" I asked. "I told him that, with medical reports upmost in everyone's mind, I must surely rule myself out," he said. He paused for effect. I had no idea what he was referring to. He finally continued, "I told him, 'After all, George, you have to remember that, because of my cancer operation twenty-five years ago, I have only one ball.'" To which George McGovern replied, "You know, Frank, that's precisely the thing that's wrong around here. There are too damn many balls in Washington."

In the summer of 1971, Amy and I sailed around the world on a tanker. We set off from Portland, Maine, and arrived sixty-seven days later in El Segundo, California. Over this period, we were on land for a grand total of about ten hours in the little Persian Gulf country of Bahrain. We brought five suitcases of books with us, and one of clothes. Every night I read out loud to Amy. We read *The Iliad, The Odyssey, The Magic Mountain, Ulysses.* It was an enchanted summer. Amy studied French and discovered Chaucer. I welcomed the expanse of unscheduled time as a second opportunity to pick up an undergraduate education. By the end of the summer I was no longer thinking of law school or the Peace Corps, or even of the end of the world. Every evening Amy and I went out on the deck and watched the sunset. Every night we looked at the stars. There was something grand about the universe and our own little corner of it that I had never really noticed before. During that summer, I firmly committed myself to a career in religion.

When we returned in September, we spent one more year in the Bay area. We returned to Stanford. I worked at Memorial Church as assistant to Davie Napier, the dean of the chapel there. In my spare time I took courses in Latin and Greek. Still making up for lost time, I also read Greek philosophy, beginning with the pre-Socratics and dutifully plodding my way through all of Plato and most of Aristotle. We lived in a little cottage on campus. I even had a couple of disciples. I am not sure what I had to teach them, other than to model a determined intensity. I was up every morning at five. By the end of the year, I was gaunt, even a bit forbidding, in appearance. At six feet two, I weighed 140 pounds, wore loose khaki clothing, and modeled a full, red, and ragged Cossack beard.

During the summer of 1972, Amy completed her undergraduate degree at Stanford with an intensive course in Latin. By now, we both knew what we wanted to be. We wanted to be scholars. And so, that September, the two of us set off for Harvard.

4. Boston

1972-1978

From the age of fourteen, Frank Church knew just what he wanted to be when he grew up. He wanted to be a United States senator. More precisely, he wanted to be chairman of the Foreign Relations Committee. In 1970, two years before I left the Bay Area, I was twenty-one years old. I had just gotten married, and I had not the faintest idea what I wanted to be when I grew up. Understandably, in looking at myself, especially when I compared myself to my father, I was not at all impressed. It was not that I regretted any past decisions. It was simply that I had no sense of future direction.

In part, I blamed my parents. Everything had come easily for me. I had never been pressured to excel. They had indulged me, and I had indulged myself. I had never been lacking in intensity, but had been mercurial in my passions and without discipline in their pursuit. During my graduate school years, all of this began to change.

My guess is that I would have made an absolute commitment to whatever I happened to be doing at this juncture in my life. Fortunately, from my present vantage point at least, the field that invited my endeavor was the study of religion. My year at the Pacific School of Religion provided me with a solid introduction to biblical studies, church history, and ethics. Our summer on the tanker gave me the opportunity to build upon what I had learned there, and fired me with a passion to learn more. When I returned to Stanford, I committed myself to the goal of becoming a great scholar of religion. I am not sure whether greatness, scholarship, or religion was the principal incentive, but for much of the next six years I devoted myself, with some small success and much personal gratification, to this end.

In the spring of 1972, Amy and I applied for graduate study to Harvard and Yale divinity schools. When both accepted us, we went east to visit Cambridge and New Haven in order to choose between the two of them. It was the week after Easter. When we arrived in Boston, our plane had to circle the airport for an hour while they cleared snow from the runway. We took the subway to Harvard Square, bought two pairs of rubber galoshes at Woolworth's, and then trudged across Harvard Yard to the Divinity School.

Our arrival on the scene as prospective students could not have made less of an impression. One fellow in the main office did bestir himself sufficiently to ask us for a fifty-dollar down payment to hold our places for admission in the fall. We asked about housing and were told that we would have to fend for ourselves. That was the end of our interview. Otherwise we were completely ignored. We walked about the campus, somewhat in awe of the general austerity of the place. Most of the students we caught any glimpse of were angular and wan in appearance. Part of it, I am sure, was the weather. They walked with their heads down to protect themselves from the elements. But there was something else as well, a kind of stark self-reliance. No one greeted us. They did not even seem to greet one another. They all seemed driven and preoccupied, lost in themselves, and in a great hurry to get wherever they were going.

Early the next morning we boarded a train for New Haven. As the train traveled south, the weather improved. The sky cleared. The snow disappeared. When we arrived at the Yale Divinity School, a group of students greeted us warmly. They took us to the admissions office, where we could not have been treated more kindly. Of course they knew who we were. We were the Churches from California. The people at Yale were gracious in response to the prospect of our coming to study there. Yes, there was ample and relatively inexpensive student housing. The married students had their own apartment building right there on campus. The emphasis at Yale was on community. We were assured that we would be very well taken care of. From our single day's visit, I was confident that this would indeed have been the case.

That evening we returned to San Francisco. For an hour or so we sat next to one another in silence, having a drink on the plane, pondering the decision we now had to make. Finally, I said, "Well, Amy, what do you think?"

"I really think we ought to go to Harvard," she replied.

Actually, Amy and I were leaning strongly toward Harvard before our trip East. During her final year at Stanford, Amy took a wonderful religion course called "From Augustine to Luther," which was taught by Heiko Oberman, a visiting professor from Tübingen who had spent several years teaching church history at Harvard Divinity School. One afternoon he invited the two of us to tea. We told him of our plans, and he strongly advised us to choose Harvard over Yale. "For one thing," he said, "they have an especially gifted professor of Latin and Greek whose name is Ralph Lazarro.

He will coax these languages out of you as if you had known them all your lives. For another, George Huntston Williams is there. That, in and of itself, is reason enough to choose Harvard."

Only later did we discover that Heiko Oberman had left the Harvard faculty because he and George Williams, each of whom has a strong personality and a distinctive view of history, could not co-exist in the same department. The school was far too small for two giants to cultivate the same field. On the other hand, years later when Timothy George of Louisville Baptist Seminary and I edited George Williams's *Festschrift*, a collection of essays written in his honor on the occasion of Williams's sixty-fifth birthday, it was Heiko Oberman who served as our sponsor. *Continuity and Discontinuity in Christianity*, our book honoring Williams, was published in Oberman's series, "Studies in the History of Christian Thought." There was one other aspect of Oberman's initial advice that significantly shaped my later life and career. Ralph Lazarro and George Williams turned out to be Unitarians.

Amy and I agree that the next two years were in many ways the most strenuous of our lives. We did almost nothing other than attend classes and study. In a desperate attempt to make up for lost time, I studied five languages at once. It was a heady, if draining experience. Two years later, I was graduated *magna cum laude* and accepted into doctoral programs in church history at Harvard, Oxford, and Cambridge. Amy earned a Master of Theological Studies with a major in medieval church history. We decided to stay at Harvard. It was the summer of 1974.

In 1974, Frank Church was involved in his third race for reelection to the Senate. Much had changed between us. My studies in history and ethics at Harvard led me to appreciate the way in which my father lived and

93

served according to a set of principles far higher than the norm. In addition, I was much more at peace with myself, which made it easier for me to affirm my parents and the things they stood for without sacrificing some fundamental part of my own identity. Though they did not ask me to, I willingly volunteered to return to Idaho with Amy and spend the summer campaigning for my father's reelection.

As it turned out, this proved to be important. It was Watergate summer. With the threat of possible impeachment hearings hanging over Washington, Senator Church was held close to his post. For nearly three weeks in late July and early August, Amy and I fulfilled my father's political commitments in Idaho. When he returned to the state with my mother, we continued to campaign on our own. We visited thirty-three of Idaho's forty-four counties. We rode in endless parades, made dozens of visits to local stations and newspapers, and shook thousands of hands at local rodeos and county fairs.

Again, the John Birch Society was active in Idaho. They distributed door to door more than a hundred thousand pamphlets entitled "Frank Church: The Chameleon in the Senate." It was the most extensive political blitz in the history of the state. Nearly four out of every five Idaho households were hit with this sixteen-page rehearsal of Church's political sins. It was a slick, if bombastic, piece of propaganda. "Did you know," the inside cover asks, "Frank Church is so pro-Communist that the Reds in Vietnam taunted our tortured P.O.W.s with his speeches? . . . Did you know the top assistant to Senator Church has been a national officer of at least two officially cited Communist Fronts? . . . Did you know Frank Church has sneered at American mothers as multiplying 'like a malignant tumor in its terminal phase,' and has threatened Americans with 'compulsory birth control'?"

As in 1968, the Birch Society saw a rare opportunity in Idaho. In 1972, John Schmitz, the right-wing presidential candidate on the American Party ticket, won his largest vote in Idaho, almost 10 per cent. The attack they mounted two years later against Church could by no means be dismissed.

The method employed was an old one. Alan Stang, the author, took Church's statements out of context. His article, reprinted from *American Opinion* magazine, opens with an attempt to discredit Church's early stand against the war in Vietnam by making him appear hypocritical. It quotes Church as saying in a 1965 speech that America's "commitments solemnly made must be kept, whether made wisely or unwisely." However, the next sentence in this speech is conveniently omitted: "But there never, at any time, has been any commitment on the part of the United States to fight the war in South Vietnam. It is the kind of war that can only be won by the South Vietnamese themselves." As columnist Jack Anderson was to comment, "This is a little like quoting Abe Lincoln as saying he would carry on his work 'with malice,' without adding the words 'toward none.'"

Another of the tactics was to spotlight issues upon which the people of Idaho were not conversant, using this method to create a climate of uncertainty about Church's true political character. A young volunteer of ours was handing out bumper stickers in the parking lot of Boise stadium one Saturday afternoon before a football game. One exchange reported to my father's aide, Loch Johnson, was typical of the problem. The driver of a pickup truck refused to take a Church sticker, but accepted one for Democratic gubernatorial candidate Cecil Andrus. Andrus, who would later serve as Secretary of the Interior in the Carter administration, was immensely popular in Idaho. As the truck pulled out, the driver's buckskin-clad wife leaned out the window and taunted the young volunteer, saying, "How can a sweet gal like you be for Church? Are you really for Church?"

"Sure. What's wrong with him?" replied the coed.

"Have you heard of the Seabed Treaty! You better look into that Church. He's just like Nelson Rockefeller. They're both out to destroy this country."

Church decided to remain above the fray. It was left to the Idaho news media to set the record straight. He did come out and defend his chief of staff, Verda Barnes, against the accusation that she was a Communist sympathizer, but beyond this he made light of the attacks. Church even ignored the fact that his opponent, while publicly on record as unsympathetic to the Birch Society effort, continued to fan the flames. By the last week in October, private polls showed that Church's twenty-point lead had all but evaporated. He was in real danger of being defeated.

Church's opponent was a Methodist minister, Robert Smith. A self-avowed Libertarian, Smith had served as administrative assistant to Idaho Congressman Steve Symms, the man who was to unseat Church six years later. "Who is Bob Smith?" his bumper stickers read. The question was never really answered. Because Smith was unknown to the people of Idaho, his campaign was fashioned as a referendum on Church. After nearly a year of negative publicity, the strategy seemed to be working. People were openly asking, if the things being circulated about Church are untrue, why is he so reluctant to respond to them?

Three days before the election, Church finally did respond. In an hour-long statewide live television broadcast, wearing the identification bracelet of an Idaho prisoner of war, one by one Church answered the various attacks on his integrity, character, and patriotism. The same points were underscored in a series of hurriedly drafted newspaper advertisements. Taken together, the dual thrust of this last-minute rebuttal may fairly be credited with turning around a faltering campaign. Church defeated his opponent by 26,000 votes out of 255,000 cast.

Amy and I returned to Harvard in the fall. I began my doctoral work. In midyear, Amy was tapped as acting dean of students at the Divinity School. She was then twenty-four. As such, she was one of a handful of women deans at Harvard, and by far the youngest. One of the perquisites of her position was a charming carriage house, conveniently located on Francis Avenue directly across from the Divinity School.

Among the first things Amy did as dean of students was to place high priority upon greeting prospective students, hoping to ensure that they would be met more graciously than we had been when we first arrived at Harvard. I always wondered a little about this. If we had been treated too kindly when we first arrived, I am not sure whether we would have considered the school sufficiently rigorous for us!

During my years at Harvard, George Huntston Williams was my principal adviser. My master's thesis, directed by Williams, was on Thomas Jefferson's Bible, *The Life and Morals of Jesus of Nazareth.* This was the same book that my father had given me when he first went to the Senate, and in it, as a graduate student in religion, I began to discover my own faith. Looking back, I can see that it was only natural that I should study the religious views of my father's political hero. Thomas Jefferson became our common ground.

Jefferson was in spirit and occasionally by claim a Unitarian. Near the end of his life, he went so far as to predict "that the present generation will see Unitarianism become the general religion of the United States." As he and others fashioned a new experiment in democracy, so they believed that a new religious order would soon follow. If our country was founded on the principles of liberty, tolerance, and reason, a new religion would surely emerge in America which would embody these same principles. It is no accident that among the founders of our country such people as Thomas Jefferson and John Adams considered themselves Unitarians. Unitarianism was a new faith for a new age.

The essence of Unitarianism, as understood by Jefferson and true to this very day, is that ethics are the essence of religion. In editing the scriptures, Jefferson emphasized Jesus' ethical teachings by striking out such things as the virgin birth and the resurrection. "My religious reading has long been confined to the moral branch of religion, which is the same in all religions; while in that which consists of dogmas, all differ," Jefferson wrote. "The former instructs us how to live well and worthily in society; the latter are made to interest our minds in the support of teachers who inculcate them."

Over time I have come to believe that there is far more variety even in the moral branch of religion than Jefferson acknowledged, and far more meaning in the ancient legends and stories than he would credit, but the point he makes here still rings true to me. When it comes to theology or matters of being and destiny, Jefferson believed as do most Unitarians today, that each individual should be free to develop and profess his or her own beliefs without coercion. To insist that one human being take on faith the revelation purportedly received by another is an unreasonable thing to ask. It follows that no single group believing in a particular revelation can lay claim to public authority, especially that of the state. In fact, any religion that has to be protected by a secular escarpment in order to flourish is ultimately destined to perish. "It is error alone which needs the support of government," Jefferson wrote. "Truth can stand by itself."

From my present vantage point, as I look back on

many of Jefferson's opinions about religion, I find them honest and bracing but lacking in imagination. He had far greater faith than I do in the power of sheer rationality as an elixir for all our ills. On the other hand, Jefferson's Bible was a bridge for me to the "unexpurgated" text, which today I much prefer, and the spirit of Unitarianism, with its emphasis on ethics and freedom, is with me still. As I struggle to find meaning in the Jewish and Christian texts I treasure, I give thanks for that gift my father gave me so many years ago, and for the way George Williams at Harvard made it come alive for me.

George Williams did far more than encourage me in my studies of Thomas Jefferson's religious thought, however. He also helped me to appreciate religious views different from my own. As Heiko Oberman predicted, the moment I got to Harvard I was drawn to George Williams, and through him I was led to Unitarianism. One of the things that so attracted me was his celebration of pluralism. Here was a Unitarian who believed in the trinity, a Protestant who considered the Pope the head of Christendom, and a Christian who held not only that Jerusalem was the holiest of cities, but also that it belonged unequivocally and forever to the Jews.

My father, too, was fascinated by Williams. I can remember a long evening's discussion between the two of them, during which many things that Williams had to say about ancient history struck home. In fact, shortly thereafter, one theme that Williams identified as recurring throughout the ages was to emerge as the cornerstone of Church's own critique of corporate and governmental lawlessness during his investigations of the multinational corporations and of the American intelligence agencies.

"George Williams, one of the much beloved professors of theology at Harvard Divinity School, once said to me something that I have always remembered," Church said during an interview for *Parade* magazine in 1975. " 'Choose your enemy very carefully, for you will grow to be more like him.' After World War II the Soviet Union became our received enemy and we undertook to contest with the Russians everything in the world. To justify emulating their method we said we had to treat fire with fire. And in the process, of course, we've become more like them. In a free society that can go only so far. We become our own worst enemy if we bring down a free society in the very name of defending it."

Church applied Williams's principle first to illegal and immoral corporate business practices abroad. In 1975, he conducted the first in-depth investigation of illicit connections between multinational corporations and foreign governments. In a series of blockbuster revelations, his Subcommittee on Multinational Corporations exposed the following: Exxon parceling out $27 million in illegal political contributions in Italy in return for economic favors from the government; Gulf Oil doling out $4 million in illegal corporate contributions in Korea; Northrop paying an agent $450,000 for the purpose of bribing Saudi Arabian generals; United Fruit slipping the president of Honduras $1.2 million to lower the export tax on bananas; Lockheed making illegal payments to government officials in countries around the globe— in Europe, in Asia, in the Middle East, and in the Far East—amounting in the aggregate to many millions of dollars. In addition, Church released a complete list of U.S. firms on the Arab boycott list.

Overseas, the impact of these revelations was staggering. Church's name was a household word in Europe and the Far East. Governments fell in Italy and Japan. The royal family of the Netherlands was rocked by allegations that Prince Bernhard had received over a million dollars in "unofficial payments" from Lockheed.

Here at home, there was a different specter, that of corporate executives upon the witness stand uncomfortably confessing the truth of Church's findings. There was a notable lack of contrition. As Church noted at the time, "All of this wrongdoing is acknowledged by straight-faced executives who say they had to break the law in order to get the business. The excuse, after all, is written plainly in the adage, 'When in Rome . . .' But the excuse is hollow. The bad habits of Rome were brought home to America. The roster of companies that made illegal corporate contributions to the Nixon campaign in 1972 includes many of the companies which have turned to bribery abroad. If we condone bribery of foreign officials we will sow the seeds of corruption in our own land." Again, the Williams principle pertains here. In Church's own words, "We must never accede to the rationale, in foreign policy or in business, that we must become as corrupt as those we come up against."

The bridge from Church's chairmanship of the Multinational Subcommittee to that of the Senate Select Committee on Intelligence was his investigation of ITT's secret offering to the CIA of a million dollars to prevent Salvador Allende, lawfully elected by the people of Chile, from becoming president. Church's growing expertise in this area, together with his persistence in ferreting out the facts, won him his next appointment. As Jerome Levenson, chief counsel for the Multinational Subcommittee, observed, "Church knew they weren't going to do a damn thing on [CIA Director Richard] Helms or [Secretary of State Henry] Kissinger, but he pushed it. The rest of the committee just wanted it all to go away. He was the only guy who pressed on. All that about Helms's meeting with ITT's [Harold] Geneen, none of that would have come out if we hadn't pressed Helms and crew. The State Department and everyone was urging him to stop and he just blasted them all to get where we did. The net plus is we exposed as issues things that had previously been sacrosanct."

Church's single most important and sensitive assignment during his twenty-four years in the Senate was the chairmanship of the Senate Select Committee on Intelligence. When asked whether he hoped that this assignment would launch him into the forefront of 1976 presidential politics, he noted, realistically, that the investigation would be "a political mine field." On the one hand, liberals and radicals were very suspicious of a "whitewash." On the other, many conservatives charged that such an investigation would weaken the CIA and diminish America's global power. "It's not at all clear that the public will fully appreciate the need for an investigation of this kind," Church said in May of 1975, just after the committee's work had begun. "It's necessary for us to look very closely and critically at some of the activities of the CIA and FBI and other agencies," particularly covert activities of the sort that had been "glamorized after a whole generation of a constant diet on television of Missions Impossible."

Church was not the only one investigating the intelligence agencies in 1975. Vice President Nelson Rockefeller was commissioned by Gerald Ford to look into charges, first made by *New York Times* reporter Seymour Hersh, that the CIA had violated its charter by carrying out extensive domestic surveillance during the late sixties and early seventies against antiwar activists and dissidents. As the investigation developed, allegations in the press of CIA assassination plots against Cuba's Fidel Castro, the Dominican Republic's Rafael Trujillo, and Vietnam's Ngo Dinh Diem broadened the circle of inquiry. When Rockefeller released his report, however, it contained nothing about assassination plots. Rockefeller said that his commission did not have enough time to look into the allegation thoroughly. "We didn't feel we could come to a conclusion on partial information," the Vice President explained.

"When we went to see Rockefeller," Church reported at the time, "it was the most beautiful finesse you ever saw. My, how glad he was to see me. My, how honored he was at my visit. And when we asked him for all of the transcripts, he understood why we wanted them and agreed it would expedite our hearings." Then, Church said, the Vice President said no, and passed the buck back.

Upon publishing his report, the Vice President assured the American public that the CIA's transgressions were "not major." Senator Church disagreed. He said that he and Rockefeller both had hard evidence of CIA assassination plots. Church preferred the word murder. "I don't regard murder plots as a minor matter," Church said. "Ours is not a wicked country and we cannot abide a wicked government." In an interview with Christopher Lydon for *The New York Times*, Church underscored this point, saying, "You know, they're trying to compare it now with the idea of doing away with Hitler in the late thirties. But we're dealing here with little countries who couldn't possibly menace the United States, whose leaders were simply inconvenient—nuisances! If we're going to lay claim to being a civilized country we must make certain in the future that no agency of our government can be licensed to murder. The President of the United States cannot become a glorified godfather."

The last week of November 1975, the Church committee released its findings on CIA assassination plots. Drawing on nearly ten thousand pages of sworn testimony taken from more than a hundred witnesses over sixty days of closed-door hearings, the report outlined five CIA attempts, all unsuccessful, upon the lives of foreign leaders. In addition to Castro, Trujillo, and Diem, the agency had also targeted the Congo's Patrice

Lumumba and General René Schneider of Chile. Earlier in his investigation, Church had characterized the CIA as a "rogue elephant" very possibly acting without presidential sanction in these cases, but the report indicates the strong possibility of at least implicit approval from the White House. While there was no hard evidence that Presidents Eisenhower, Kennedy, and Johnson—or their close advisers—had authorized these plots, the report concluded that "as Chief Executive Officer of the United States each must bear the ultimate responsibility for the activities of his subordinates."

On the other hand, the methods used by the CIA in these attempts, as well as its agents' ineptitude in carrying them out, did expose the agency to some ridicule. There was a kind of amateurish James Bond quality about its exploits. In the case of Castro, for instance, there were poison cigars, skin-diving suits dusted with lethal powder, even seashells charged with explosives to be laced in Castro's favorite diving grounds.

The committee was unanimous in its findings. Columnist Mary McGrory wrote, "The only people who come unscathed out of the Church Committee report, 'Alleged Assassination Plots Involving Foreign Leaders,' are the people who wrote it—the chairman, his colleagues and the staff." Republican senators Barry Goldwater of Arizona and John Tower of Texas did issue a minority report dissenting to its publication. "The wholesale foraging of the Congress into the details of foreign policy and the intelligence services upon which it depends can only serve to give comfort to our opponents and to embarrass our friends," Goldwater said.

Church disagreed. "A basic tenet of our democracy is that the people must be told of the mistakes of their government so that they may have the opportunity to correct them. We believe that foreign peoples will, upon sober reflection, admire our nation more for keeping faith with our democratic ideals than they will condemn us for the misconduct itself. Moreover, whatever the possible short-term detriment to our reputation abroad, it will be far outweighed by the constructive result at home of enabling the American people to fully understand what was done secretly in their name. Revealing the truth will strengthen our political system, which depends upon an informed public, and will help reestablish the trust of the American people in the candor of their government."

Church had always been an idealist and, like every idealist, he ran the risk of being labeled naive. His main concern was that any compromise on fundamental American principles, especially if hidden from the people themselves, could lead to a gradual erosion of the moral foundation of our republic. "The United States must not adopt the tactics of the enemy," he wrote in his introduction to the committee's report on assassinations. "Means are as important as ends. Crisis makes it tempting to ignore the wise restraints that make men free; but each time we do so, each time the means we use are wrong, our inner strength, the strength which makes us free, is lessened."

There are two dangers here. One was, again, the Williams principle. Regardless of how great our internal freedoms were in comparison with those of the Soviet Union, if we imitated the Soviets in our covert adventures abroad peoples throughout the world would perceive little difference between us. The other danger was perhaps even more insidious. With the advent of modern technology, the same devices that were now being employed in intelligence gathering overseas could be turned upon our own citizenry here at home.

Church's concerns were supported by hard facts. Among the abuses of power within the intelligence services uncovered during the course of his investigation were the use by the Internal Revenue Service of a staff to gather intelligence on American citizens simply because they disagreed politically with the Nixon administration; the illegal accumulation by the CIA of 7,200 files on American citizens because they dissented on the Vietnam war; and illegal mail-opening programs by the CIA directed against Americans between 1940 and 1973. In his own file, Church was surprised to find a letter that he had written to his mother-in-law from Moscow in 1971.

Church got generally high marks for the way he conducted his investigation of the intelligence agencies. One reporter, writing for the Washington *Star*, groused, "Church is going about his investigation with a seriousness that is almost oppressive. His committee has been the most leak proof in memory and he talks with furrowed brow and half-closed eyes about his determination to avoid jumping to judgment on a matter of gravity." Unlike a parallel investigation in the House, Church's operation was in fact almost entirely free of leaks.

Occasionally, Church's penchant for colorful rhetoric got the better of him. The "rogue elephant" remark proved unfortunate. He also got a little carried away during the first public hearing with CIA Director William Colby, seizing the occasion to brandish a lethal dart gun in a classic "photo opportunity" for the press. Nonetheless, Church made it through the mine field relatively unscathed. On the other hand, far from launching his presidential candidacy, the Intelligence Committee investigation simply delayed it. He refused to begin his campaign until the proceedings were finished. By the time they were, in March of 1976, it was too late for him to mount a fully financed campaign. Despite his late inning successes, including victories in four primaries and one caucus state, by the time Church entered the campaign for the presidency, Jimmy Carter had built a commanding lead, which neither Church nor the other late entrant, Governor Jerry Brown of California, could overcome.

Two months before Church was tapped for the Intelligence Committee post, he had decided to test the presidential waters. He had formed a committee to explore the possibility of his running only to disband it when the investigation began. About the same time, there was a flurry of cover stories featuring Church's presidential prospects. One question that kept being asked was whether Church was too much of a boy scout to be considered seriously for the presidency.

"In a time of disgust with politicians, in a time when people are frightened about the economy and their own future, could a public used to saber-rattling Presidents rally behind a Gentleman candidate?" one reporter asked. "Could another Mr. Nice Guy be offered up by the Democrats so soon after 1972's Mr. Nice Guy debacle?"

Senator Gary Hart, the director of McGovern's campaign, a member of Church's Intelligence Committee, and, like Church, later regarded as a somewhat enigmatic loner in the Senate, thought for a moment and replied, "Have the people had it with a 'good guy'? First, this town is not 'people.' If you mean the country, the answer is no! The trouble is, good guys seldom get a chance to be known in the country because they seldom get a chance to emerge out of this sink hole. Church is not a member of a clique. He is decent and independent. He does not stab people in the back. He's not scrambling up other people's backs."

George McGovern himself was not sure. "I'm afraid there is some truth that he may suffer from the too-nice of a guy image . . . But there have been presidents who were quiet, restrained people. Who? Well, Thomas Jefferson for one. I think Frank Church is capable of writing things as eloquent as Jefferson or Lincoln. He's very effective on everything he's ever done."

Shortly before his announcement, Church's first gambit as a prospective candidate was reminiscent of the first time he tried to preside over the Foreign Relations Committee nearly twenty years before. He was at a fund raiser at Senator Claiborne Pell's home in Washington, and the press was invited. As reported the following day in the Washington *Post*, Pell hopped onto a sofa in his living room, balanced himself deftly as he sank into the soft cushions, and introduced the man he hoped would be the next President. Church then attempted the same maneuver. He climbed up, sank into the treacherous underfooting, fought unsuccessfully to gain his balance, and, while pitching forward, reached the obvious conclusion, "Wait, I can't stand on it." Successful in his second try, Church straightened up and announced wryly, "That, my friends, must be a Republican platform."

At the same party, Church joked about his late start. He observed that his wife, Bethine, was wearing jewelry in the shape of a turtle around her neck. "That's the symbol of our campaign," he said. He also pulled out a "Grin and Bear It" cartoon relating how Senator Snort, in his own presidential campaign, had saved the public thousands of dollars in the cost of Secret Service protection by declaring late.

Two days later, on March 18, 1976, Church was back in Idaho. "The best roads in life lead home again." Standing on the steps of the historic red brick courthouse in Idaho City, Idaho, Frank Church announced his candidacy for President. This was the same frontier mining town where his grandfather had first settled during the gold rush, where his father was born before Idaho had yet become a state, and where his father-in-law had declared his candidacy for governor. Church was only the

second Idahoan in history to run for President. His boyhood hero, Senator William Borah, had declared the
same lofty goal forty years before.

Church's supporters, many of them clad in blue jeans
and wearing cowboy hats and cowboy boots, went wild.
More than two thousand of them cheered and waved
placards that read: RETURN TO GREATNESS, and A TIME FOR
OLD-FASHIONED HONESTY—CHURCH FOR PRESIDENT. "The
pioneers of the early west were men and women of un-
common strength and faith," Church said. "They had
the strength to endure the hardships of life in the wilderness. And they had faith enough in themselves and the
future to overcome their fears."

Much of Church's announcement was a point-by-
point rendition of the liberal agenda, complete with a
few of the "small is better" twists that distinguished the
new Democratic rhetoric from that of the Great Society
days. Church opened and closed, however, with his one
distinctive and most cherished theme.

"It is a leadership of weakness and fear which insists
that we must imitate the Russians in our treatment of
foreign peoples, adopting their methods of bribery,
blackmail, abduction, and coercion, as if they were our
own. And it is a leadership of weakness and fear which
permits the most powerful agencies of our government
—the CIA, the FBI, and the IRS—to systematically ignore the very laws intended to protect the liberties of the
people. These are crimes against freedom."

It was 1976, the Bicentennial year. Church's obligatory
invocation of the Founding Fathers called forth the vision of a very different America from that traditionally
celebrated in Fourth of July speeches. "In stark contrast
with contemporary Presidents, our Founding Fathers
were a different breed," Church proclaimed. "They
acted on their faith, not their fear. They did not believe
in fighting fire with fire; crime with crime; evil with evil;

or delinquency by becoming delinquents. They set themselves against the terrors of a totalitarian state by structuring a government that would obey the law. They knew that the only way to escape a closed society was to accept the risk of living in an open one."

I was sitting on the platform with Amy, my mother, and my brother. It was a beautiful spring morning, the streets muddy following a brief thunder shower, the sun breaking through the clouds. With the picturesque backdrop of century-old wooden churches and saloons, with people outstretched through the streets as far as the eye could see, Frank Church spoke to the people of Idaho of his vision for America's role in a changing world.

"I would call for a discriminating foreign policy which recognizes that the postwar period is over; that we are no longer the one rich patron of a war-wrecked world. We should continue to stand fast in those places, like Western Europe and the Middle East, where our stakes are large, but there is no justification any longer for us to subsidize half a hundred foreign governments scattered all over the globe. In Africa and Asia, new societies are emerging from the grip of nineteenth-century colonialism. This Third World will be filled with revolution and upheaval for the balance of this century. A volcano cannot be capped. The United States can abide much ferment in distant places. But we cannot successfully serve as trustee for the broken empires of Europe."

It was a far cry from Church's cold-war rhetoric in the keynote speech sixteen years before. Then, expressing his full allegiance to the prevailing philosophy of the times, Church spoke of "the fraternity of the free." Now, with no less flourish, he declaimed, "the foreign policy of this country must be wrested from the hands of that fraternity of compulsive interventionists who have involved us in so many futile foreign wars! I reject the siege mentality that kept us locked so long in the straitjacket of the cold war, and I would work diligently to bring an end to the insanity of the nuclear arms race which makes both sides potential targets for mutual extinction.

"There are those, I know, who say it is too late to enter the race for the presidency," Church concluded. "To those who say it is too late, I reply that it's never too late —nor are the odds ever too great—to try. In that spirit the west was won, and in that spirit I now declare my candidacy for President of the United States."

No one took Church's chances very seriously. "Enter Frank Cathedral," *Newsweek* magazine announced, a headline representing an upgrade from the days that Lyndon Johnson called Church "Frank Sunday School," but little more. Columnist Jack Anderson, calling Church a man of courage and decency, welcomed Church's candidacy, as did *The New York Times*, stating that "in terms of the nation's self-education on the issues, the Church candidacy can only be a positive event." In general, however, the race seemed set. Governor Jimmy Carter had outdistanced what had been a large field. Representative Morris Udall was still in the race, but had yet to win a primary. And compared to Carter's, Church's treasury of less than half a million dollars was a pittance.

Church set up shop in Washington at 410 First Street, the modest offices where George McGovern had launched his 1972 campaign. In gathering his campaign staff, Church looked to family and old friends. Carl Burke, his oldest friend, was named campaign manager. In his first day on the job, Burke recalled the night in 1956 when he and Frank Church emerged from the Boise cellar where they had been cranking out notices of Church's candidacy for the Senate. Church said to him then, "Well, Burke, we've crossed the Rubicon."

Church himself, in a conversation with Jack Anderson, recalled not his first campaign but his struggle with cancer: "After that experience, I decided that life itself was a major risk. It could be snatched away at any moment. It has to be lived to the fullest. I had to take big chances. Win or lose, I had to play for high stakes."

Our old family friend Henry Kimelman, who had served as finance director for the McGovern presidential campaign, assumed the same position in Church's campaign staff. Church then named Bill Landau, a Republican accountant from New York, as his treasurer. He joked that he wanted to make sure that the campaign would stay out of debt. It did. My best friend and high school classmate, Peter Fenn, who had worked on the Intelligence Committee, was made a field officer. I was dispatched to Nebraska, the first state we would contest, as codirector of the effort there with Idaho rancher Joe McCarter.

When it became clear that my father would throw his hat into the presidential ring, I petitioned for a leave of absence from my studies at Harvard. This was not officially granted. I was told that if I left the program, it was possible that I would have to reapply for admission. It was hard to believe that they were serious, but the director of my program seemed deadly earnest. The fate of my student career was of little consequence, however, compared to my father's quest.

By March I was in Nebraska. On the day I arrived a local poll was published in the Omaha *World*. We were in seventh place, at a statistically meaningless one per cent. To complicate matters further, the Republican Secretary of State had placed Hubert Humphrey's and Ted Kennedy's names on the ballot. I remembered something that theologian Peter Berger once had written: "Angels can fly because they take themselves lightly." Given the odds, that seemed the way to go.

Over the next ten weeks I visited every county in

Nebraska. I dropped by every local newspaper, every radio station, every television studio. I gave pep talks to our hardy band of followers. I did what I could to secure endorsements from local political leaders whose candidates had dropped out of the race. And I set up a twelve-day campaign swing, a bus trip covering the state, for my father.

The bus trip was emblematic of our down-home low budget campaign. Eastern reporters unfortunate enough to be assigned to Church's campaign suffered a certain amount of culture shock. Typical of the coverage is this description of the Church campaign that ran in *Time* magazine on May 3.

> Church is in search of the "folks" as he put it, and they are not always easy to find in the great open spaces. In one hour's stretch, while campaigning in Nebraska, his caravan came across a herd of antelope, some buffalo, and two horsemen who were moving too fast to be approached. There was not a single human hand to grasp until he reached the "cowboy capital" of Ogallala (pop. 4,976) . . . As the chartered bus chugged along a Nebraska road, a jackrabbit darted out from the underbrush and ran by its side. For a while the race was close, but the bus finally gained on the hare and outdistanced him. Inside the bus, Presidential Candidate Frank Church chuckled over the good omen—"The tortoise is doing it again!"

Indeed, Church did appear to be gaining in the polls. Jimmy Carter changed his campaign plans and made a brief swing through Nebraska right before the primary. Their only meeting was at the Jefferson-Jackson Day dinner in Omaha four days before the election. Carter was not expected to attend. He did not "want to be a spoiler," his state campaign coordinator said. Right after Church finished his speech, however, Lieutenant Governor Gerald Whelan announced, with some irritation, that although he had "understood" that Carter was not coming to the dinner, he was in fact in the hall. One reporter noted that "even Carter's partisans were a little taken aback by the thunder-stealing attempt and could only raise a tentative cheer."

Carter went on to call Church a "fine young man." Both of them were fifty-one. He also noted that his "very good friend" had made "a remarkably fine speech." He had not heard it, he admitted, but he could "tell from the applause." By the time Carter had finished, one of Church's staffers had managed to collect a bucket of potatoes, which Church then presented to Carter, calling them Idaho peanuts. It was a master stroke, well deserved given the circumstances, and the foolish sort of thing that helps to win elections.

Church's strategy was to put together a liberal coalition of Kennedy, Humphrey, Bayh, Harris, and Udall supporters. All of them were on the ballot in Nebraska. The goal, therefore, was to turn it into a two-man race. With an effective media campaign and nearly two weeks of personal campaigning in the state, Church managed to do just that. By election day on May 11, he beat Jimmy Carter by one percentage point. To the cheers of his supporters, Church proclaimed: "On to Oregon! On to Idaho! On to Montana!" As *Time* magazine commented in acknowledging Church's victory, "It was an unlikely game plan for a Presidential hopeful and, with the possible exception of Church himself, no one placed much faith in the Idaho senator's 'late, late strategy.' "

Despite continuing skepticism, with Church's victory in Nebraska the tone in the press began to change. *Newsweek* noted in acknowledging Church's surprise victory, "His Nebraska campaign was very nearly a mom-and-pop show—Church crossed the state by campaign bus, while his 27-year-old son, Forrest, a Unitarian minister, minded the store—but it was also shrewdly professional." Shrewdness and professionalism are things that members of the press understand and respect. I must admit, our campaign in Nebraska did not seem particularly shrewd or professional to me. It was, however, successful—the thing people seem to respect most of all —and Church, who would have dropped out of the race had he lost in Nebraska, was on his way to Oregon, still chasing the hare.

When we arrived in Oregon, Church was trailing Jimmy Carter by about 15 per cent in the polls. Oregon was familiar territory, however, and after Church's victory in Nebraska against much greater odds, he was confident. A new factor in the race was the entry of Governor Jerry Brown of California. Now Church was running against two celebrities, one on account of his front-runner status, the other due to his iconoclastic philosophy and fascinating, if angular, political style.

Whatever chances Church's "late, late strategy" had of succeeding were diminished even further by Brown's own eleventh-hour entry. There simply was not room for two tortoises in a race against the hare. Brown beat Carter in Maryland; Church beat Carter in Nebraska. In fact, between them they won eight of the final ten contested primaries. The impact either one might have had was diluted, however, by the other's presence in the race.

The race in Oregon was a fascinating one. Brown announced as a write-in candidate. Carter furiously tried to maintain his lead. All three candidates traveled throughout Oregon for the better part of a week. It was a political carnival: Brown's children's crusade and metaphysical rambling; Carter's ready smile and humorless manner; Church's ten-minute answers and a visit to the tortoise in the Portland zoo.

As the days went by, Church was beginning to get more attention in the national media. For the first time his press buses were full. When Church started out, he was likely to have a larger press contingent from Italy or Japan than he had from the United States. The victory in Nebraska changed all that. But questions about Church's candidacy continued.

Commenting on the Oregon campaign, Les Ledbetter, writing for *The New York Times*, admitted that "whether his stops have been in the conservative southern part of this state, in the coastal portion where he is now or in more liberal Portland, Senator Church has consistently received friendly welcomes and enthusiastic goodbyes. His long, detailed answers, however, have provoked disappointment among those waiting for easier, more reassuring statements, and he has sometimes failed to generate the kind of excitement that his two major opponents seem to."

The people of Oregon apparently were not put off by Church's approach. He won handily, surging in the polls during the final three days, and capturing almost half of Oregon's delegates. Church also won in his home state of Idaho, surely no surprise, although the margin, 80 per cent, gave Church a personal boost. In Nevada, which Church did not contest, Governor Brown scored decisively over Carter.

Frank Church's campaign was now launched. Money started pouring in. He was finally receiving recognition, where before he had been all but ignored.

It was interesting to observe the bewilderment on the part of many East Coast reporters and columnists as they observed Church on the campaign trail in Oregon. In Oregon I had a drink one evening with David Broder of the Washington *Post*, perhaps the most respected political analyst among the syndicated columnists. Broder admitted that he did not know my father well. This was not his fault. Church was uncomfortable in his personal dealings with the press. To the chagrin of his own press secretary, Church almost never lubricated his own way by offering reporters or columnists invitations to lunch or private consultations in his Capitol hideaway. In fact, he never got over his dislike of the telephone, which further impeded the possibility that Church might be prevailed upon to give some key reporter a friendly call.

Broder recorded his own astonishment at Church's effectiveness as a campaigner in a piece he wrote, following the Oregon primary, entitled "Frank Church: the Unbeaten Candidate." "Church obviously has his work cut out for him," Broder wrote, "but he is likely to surprise people—if the reaction of those who saw him campaigning for the first time this past week in the west is any guide. Church's reputation among those who have watched him in the Senate for almost twenty years is that of a plump, sometimes pompous, pillowfighter of a politician, who is more inclined to pummel a point to putty rather than dispatch it with a neat upper-cut. . . . The surprise was the cool, controlled and highly effective Church who could be seen both on live interviews and in filmed ads on Oregon television last week. That Church won votes."

Despite his successes in Nebraska, Oregon, and Idaho, Frank Church knew that, in order for him to have any real chance of capturing the nomination, he would have to sweep all the contests that were to take place between the Oregon primary and Super Tuesday, when California, Ohio, and New Jersey were up for grabs. Nothing less than this would fuel his campaign with sufficient funds to propel him into contention in these large and expensive states.

It was by no means impossible that Church might accomplish a sweep on June 1. The two primaries to be held on that day were Montana and Rhode Island. The caucus state was Utah. Church led in the polls in Montana. He was better organized than Carter or Brown in Utah. And in Rhode Island, he enjoyed the support of the two leading Democratic officeholders, Senator Claiborne Pell, the aristocrat of the Senate, and Congressman Ed Beard, the only blue-collar member of the House. Both Pell and Beard cut television and radio spots on Church's behalf.

With the two of them by his side, Church campaigned throughout the state. As the lesser-known candidate, in his previous victories Church had counted upon a rush of interest among the electorate just before primary day, when he and his ideas were most visible. The tag line on his commercials, in fact, spoke directly to the uninterested voter: "Frank Church. At last, a candidate who makes you want to vote." There was only one problem. It was Memorial Day weekend, and no one was paying any attention.

I was campaigning in California when I heard the results from Rhode Island on my car radio. Brown, Carter, and Church had almost evenly split the Rhode Island vote. There were just a few more than a thousand votes separating the three of them, but Brown was on top. Church took Montana and Utah handily, but the morning papers read, "Brown and Church divide primary victories." Again, the late, late candidates were successful against Carter. But the focus was blurred. Where one might have succeeded, two were bound to fail.

After Brown and Church traded victories on June 1, the following week of the campaign lost some of its momentum, despite the number of delegates involved. Due to his early successes and the steady accumulation of delegates nationwide, Jimmy Carter had the race all but sewn up.

Frank Church's efforts during this final week of campaigning comically mirrored his prospects. First, he contracted a virus and lost his voice, so had to cancel his final two days of appearances in California. Then, he flew

with his entourage to Ohio, only to discover upon land-
ing that the Teton Dam had collapsed in Idaho. Of
course, he would have to abandon campaigning and return at once to his home state. He told me on the phone
somewhat sardonically that not all was lost. At least the
national press corps was traveling with him. An hour
later, they all boarded Church's chartered jet and prepared to take off for Idaho. Just before the passenger
ramp was lifted, a "rogue" baggage truck went out of
control and smashed into the side of the plane, jamming
the lift mechanism on the ramp. Church had to charter
a tiny Lear jet. He, Bethine, one staff member, and one
CBS pool reporter, so large his knees were tucked under
his chin, flew all night and finally arrived in Idaho at
dawn to survey the damage. Frank Church's quixotic
quest for the presidency had come to a close.

In fewer than a hundred days, Frank Church had gar-
nered about 100 delegates in his race for the presidency;
1,501 delegates were required. Unlike Udall and Brown,
Church chose not to allow his name to be placed in
nomination at the Democratic Convention. He saw no
reason to prolong the inevitable. Besides, by conceding
to Carter, he might enhance his chances for the vice-
presidency.

We all gathered in Washington. With his family by his
side, and without tears, Frank Church withdrew from
the race. He wore his turtle tie. He laughed and joked
with the crowd. He offered a priceless rendition of his
final ill-starred week of campaigning. One thing was
clear to everyone there that day: Frank Church had had
a wonderful time running for President.

After the primaries, Jimmy Carter returned to Plains,
Georgia, and instituted his vice-presidential search. He
and his staff winnowed the list down to six names: Senators Adlai Stevenson III of Illinois, Henry Jackson of
Washington, Walter Mondale of Minnesota, John Glenn

of Ohio, Edmund Muskie of Maine, and Frank Church of Idaho. Congressman Peter Rodino of New Jersey was also on the list, but he withdrew, citing his age and eye trouble.

Early reports out of Plains, subsequently confirmed by Carter's top advisers, were that Church was Jimmy Carter's initial first choice. Church had proved himself on the campaign trail, something that Carter admired, even if Church's success came at his own expense. Church had run a clean race against Carter. He also offered much-needed balance to the ticket especially in the area of foreign relations, where Carter was weak. And despite his relative youthfulness, he had served in the United States Senate for twenty years.

Just before we all left for a family vacation in the Caribbean, Church received a call from ABC reporter Sam Donaldson from Plains. "What's happened?" Donaldson asked. "Yesterday, you were everyone's top pick around here, but now it appears from what I hear that you have been dropped from consideration."

Church was as bewildered as Donaldson. Judging from a recent report to Henry Kimelman, he was the first choice of Carter aides Hamilton Jordan and Morris Dees. In fact, across the board, the word we were getting out of Plains was clearly that Church was Carter's choice. Admittedly, he had yet to meet with Carter, though about a week before he had spent the afternoon with Carter's confidant, Atlanta lawyer Charles Kirbo. As far as Church could tell, it was an unexceptional if somewhat awkward meeting, though rumors out of Plains later suggested that Kirbo had not been overly impressed with Church. In addition, Church had been unwilling to change his vacation plans. He was perfectly happy to meet with Carter in New York, not in Plains. He had not taken into account the fact that Carter would likely have made his decision before convention week.

In addition to the background and health checks being made by Kirbo, Jimmy Carter had been doing his own survey of congressional leaders. Judging from various comments reported over the years, Church was likely described by certain of his colleagues as "a loner, a maverick, somewhat pretentious and aloof." His friends might have cast him as "independent, thoughtful, and somewhat shy," but whichever way you cut it, taken together these qualities hardly commended Church as a likely prospect for the second spot on the ticket. Furthermore, Hubert Humphrey, the one leader Carter was especially solicitous of cultivating, was vigorously lobbying for his old protégé, Walter Mondale. The more Church thought about it, the clearer it became that the vice-presidential nomination was never in the cards for him.

He alluded to many of these factors in an interview with Marian Christy published on August 1 in the Boston *Globe*. After turning down his offer of a cigar—"You don't want it? Well, in these days of liberation you just don't know. If I didn't make the offer, I'd be accused of chauvinism"—Christy asked Church about the vice-presidency.

"I've got enemies in high places," Church replied. "I was on a committee that exposed corruption and wrongdoing. There are certain powerful board and conference rooms where I am friendless. I have played inquisitor and inquisitors become critics. Do you know any wildly popular critics?"

In fact, Church would have been very uncomfortable as Vice President. Not only was the chemistry between him and Carter not particularly good, but he had always chafed at ceremonial roles. He would surely have become frustrated, and likely would have proved much less effective a team player than Walter Mondale did.

While it possibly played no part in Carter's decision,

there was one bizarre episode during this period that Church fixed on with a certain amount of justifiable paranoia. Its significance hit him about a week before the Democratic Convention. We were on our vacation, out on a boat in the Bahamas. My father and I were standing on the bridge one evening just after dark. All was still.

"You know," he said to me, "I have been terribly naive."

"What do you mean, Dad?"

"Just before we left Washington, I got a call from the CIA. They told me that they had received unconfirmed reports that the *Economist* magazine would be featuring an article in its October issue revealing that the Senate Intelligence Committee had been infiltrated by the KGB. At the time I thought nothing about it. I knew it was not true. The security could not have been tighter. Everyone on the committee received a top security clearance from the FBI. So I referred this matter back to a member of the staff, and thought nothing more about it."

"So?"

"So, can you imagine any rumor more certain to spook a presidential candidate than that his prospective Vice President has overseen an operation which was infiltrated by the KGB? They would not have to use it until it became clear that I was about to be chosen. Then, you can be sure that it would be part of the intelligence packet sent to Plains, if it has not been included already. You know, Forrest, this is the kind of disinformation I have been poring over ad nauseam for almost two years. I'll bet you anything that after the convention we won't hear another thing about this."

He was right. The man who was named as prospective author of this article did not even exist. In any event, there was no such article, even as there had been no KGB infiltration of the Intelligence Committee.

Church's feeling that he had been sandbagged by the

CIA might have been an illusion. One thing is certain, however. There is no member of the Senate whom the leaders of our intelligence services would have less preferred sitting a heartbeat away from the presidency, and they certainly had the means to hinder Church's ascent had they perceived a danger of his actually being chosen by Carter.

We stood out under the stars late into the evening that night. "Kismet," my father said to me. "Some things are simply meant to be or not to be. We cannot worry about them. The other things, they are the ones that matter." And then the two of us, in wistful good spirits, sang together all of the songs that we could remember from *Camelot* and *Man of La Mancha*.

When I returned to Cambridge in August, following the Democratic Convention, I had a difficult decision to make. Tim Kraft, field director of the Carter campaign, called and asked me if I would serve as Carter-Mondale state director in Nebraska.

I was sorely tempted. For one thing, I had loved the ten weeks I spent in Nebraska campaigning for my father. The whole campaign had been a heady experience for me, but Nebraska especially. Also, I was well connected there, and would be even more so following the November election. Roughly half of the Democrats in the state were partisans of my father; the other half had backed Carter in the primary. By directing the Carter effort I could expand upon my already considerable base in the state, perhaps even consider running for Congress myself in a couple of years.

I was twenty-seven years old. Kraft's offer struck me as an opportunity finally to graduate into adulthood. I had never held a real job. My wife was supporting me. I had at least two years of school ahead of me. And I loved politics.

There was one other, more negative inducement.

After six months away from my studies, Harvard was a forbidding place to return to. If my political confidence was high, my academic confidence was at an all-time low. Furthermore, there was still some question as to whether I would be welcome. Professor Williams assured me that he could smooth the feathers of the man who had authority over whether or not I would be accepted back into my program. The question was, once readmitted, could I hack it? Ahead of me lay a whole bank of written and oral exams, which I would have to pass before I could even begin my dissertation. Despite the number of years I had invested to get to this point, my future at Harvard looked bleak.

I had two weeks in which to make a decision. Every evening I convinced myself that I should forget Harvard and take the plunge into politics. Every morning I awoke possessed by doubt.

Two factors were critical in my final decision to complete my doctoral work. First, I wrote an article. For the previous six months, everywhere I went I had carted along all the basic research for an article I was writing for *Church and State* quarterly, entitled "The First American Amnesty Debate: Religion and Politics in Massachusetts, 1783–84." Again, as with my master's thesis on Thomas Jefferson, I seized on a topic that my father would find familiar and built with it a bridge back to my adopted ground. The issue was an interesting one, its question being, after the war of independence, what rights remained for those who were loyal to the King and fled to Canada? Could they return with impunity, or should they be punished for their betrayal of the revolutionary cause? In reading the sermons of the day, I discovered that Calvinist ministers generally counseled retribution. They emphasized God's justice and demanded a tooth for a tooth. In contrast, Universalist ministers recommended compassion, citing God's mercy. This

subject had meaning for me. It recalled me to my faith.
I gave myself a week. It was painful but I did it. I lost
myself in the material. I wrote the article. Now, if I were
to leave Harvard, I could do so with my academic pride
intact.

Then I called my father. He and my mother had always hoped that I would follow him into politics. For
them both, there was no more exciting or meaningful life
than a life of public service. My father did have an admi-
ration for scholars and he always regretted that his own
education had been cut short by the war. On the other
hand, he chafed at elitism of any kind, and had little
patience with ideological academicians, especially those
who were active on the public stage. He found them
precious, self-important, abstracted, and either irrelevant or dangerous. Academics such as Walt Rostow,
Henry Kissinger, and Zbigniew Brzezinski were the ar-
chitects of a global policy for America that Church
found frightening. As for me, I was involved in a field
of study, primarily the study of ancient texts, that he had
a hard time taking seriously. My first article, which was
published in the *Harvard Theological Review* in 1975, was
entitled "Sex and Salvation in Tertullian." He read it,
but it obviously meant nothing to him.

The same was true of almost everything I was doing
at Harvard. I translated a Greek word book from Ger-
man to English. And I had just completed two years of
study in Coptic, the language of Egyptian monks in the
second and third centuries. My specialty was Gnosti-
cism, which my father considered mystifying and basically irrelevant. He was pleased at my successes, but had
a hard time veiling his disappointment that I had not
chosen a more active and socially redeeming career.

When I called him on the phone, my father expressed
delight and pride upon learning that I had been asked to
run the Carter campaign in Nebraska. My mother was

ecstatic. "What should I do?" I asked. My father told me that I should not rush to a decision. He would sleep on it and get back to me in a day or two to tell me what he thought.

He called the next morning. "Forrest," he said, "you know that there is nothing that would give your mother or me more pleasure than for you to go into politics. You have a whole lifetime ahead of you, however. I have always believed that one should see through the things one begins. You have invested nearly six years in graduate school. Do what you will, but I strongly counsel you to remain at Harvard and get your degree. Then you can do anything you want. But if you do not do this, you may very well regret it for the rest of your life."

I knew that he was right. And there was one more thing. Had I gone into politics, I would not have been following my father. However fast his rise, he worked very hard to attain his success. For me, it would have been easy. I was given an opportunity to take the elevator to the fourteenth floor. From there it was a relatively short climb to the top.

Looking back, I realize that by staying at Harvard, I was not only following my father's advice, but also following much more closely in his footsteps than would have been the case had I left school and taken up politics. At Harvard, I continued to build a firm foundation for myself. Nothing came easy. Nothing was handed to me. I had to earn every honor I received. That is the way it had been for my father also. As it turns out, our chosen careers were different, but the paths we chose to follow were perhaps not as unlike as they might seem.

I stayed at Harvard and in July of 1978, I received my Ph.D. Two months later we moved to New York City, I took over as minister of All Souls Unitarian Church, and Amy and I had our first child.

5. New York

1978-1984

With all that was happening in my life during the summer of 1978, defending my doctoral dissertation, moving to New York, becoming a parish minister, one thing stands out above the others. I was about to become a father.

I remember when it finally hit me. I was at Fenway Park in Boston. I think the score was 9–7 in the fifth, typical of Fenway, which is a hitter's ballpark. Amy was with me, seven months pregnant. The night before, she had left her contact lenses in too long and had scratched her corneas, so on the way to Fenway we had to stop at the emergency room. They put some drops in Amy's eyes and put patches over them so she couldn't see even if she wanted to. She later said that it was one of the strangest afternoons she had ever spent in her entire life.

My awakening was triggered by a commonplace event. We were sitting behind a man and his son. The two of them were talking about the game. The father put his arm around his boy, and all of a sudden it struck me. I knew it in my bones. A sea change was about to take place. I too was about to become a father.

More than anything else, more than finishing my doctorate or assuming my position at All Souls, growing up surely had to do with this. I stepped up one rung on the ladder of mortality, and there was someone behind me.

Sitting in the ballpark next to my pregnant wife, I thought of my mother and father. I thought of the hopes and fears they too must have had as I slept dreamlessly in my mother's womb. From my own experience I expect that they too were struck by the mystery of creation, the miracle of childbearing, the pain and the fear, and the stunning vulnerability that comes to those who assume responsibility for bringing up children. How fragile our children are. How much it hurts us when they suffer or fail. Their vulnerability becomes our vulnerability; their pain, our pain. And no matter how much we love them, there is so very little we can do to protect them. No matter how much we give them, there is so very little that life and death cannot take away.

The first sermon I delivered at All Souls was entitled "Great Expectations." Until this very moment, seven years later, the almost ludicrous obviousness of this title had escaped me. I was talking about the church, but subconsciously my thoughts were fixed upon my unborn child.

All Souls is the oldest Unitarian church in Manhattan. The congregation was gathered in 1819, as a liberal religious alternative to the more orthodox Protestantism of the day. Nearly 160 years later, at twenty-nine years of age, I was called to serve as its ninth minister.

I had had no intention at all of going into the parish ministry. For the past eight years, my career track had been an academic one. I was ordained, having received a call to First and Second Church in Boston in 1975, but even this was primarily a teaching appointment. I had delivered only about five sermons in my entire life, and over the past year all my attention had been given to my dissertation on the Coptic Gospel of Thomas, and to an article on Paul's Letter to Philemon which was later published in the *Harvard Theological Review.*

This is not to say that I had attained my goal of becoming a great scholar. I was, however, an inventive and assiduous one. Today I cannot even read my own footnotes, but back in 1978, with more than ten articles to my credit and a promising career ahead of me, I was passionately committed to the scholarly life.

All Souls is a flagship church in the Unitarian Universalist denomination, a great historic pulpit. The search committee was working with a list of about twenty-five names. My name had not been submitted by denominational headquarters, but referred by Rhys Williams, minister of First and Second Church in Boston. Any skepticism toward me in our Department of Ministry was surely understandable. I was young and had no real parish experience. All of the other prospective candidates were in their forties and fifties. Most of them had served at least three churches, and all of them had years of hard-won experience in the ministry.

Finally, we agreed to go to New York for an interview. My friend Rhys Williams told me that, if nothing else, Amy and I would get a free weekend in the city. As it turned out, that weekend was to change our entire life.

I became a Unitarian in 1974 near the end of my second year at Harvard. The first time I entered a Unitarian church was in November of 1963. It was the River Road Unitarian Church in Bethesda, which was meeting then in my old elementary school about half a block from our house. I went to church that cold late November Sunday to hear my father deliver the sermon, a eulogy for President Kennedy, who had just been murdered in Dallas. Two days before, when the early reports of an attempted assassination came through the public address system at my high school, a number of my classmates had cheered.

On Sunday, the simple yet moving service and my father's sermon took the edge off that memory and helped me in my own grief.

My father had been raised a Catholic. He left the church when he was a teenager, but throughout his life he maintained a deep respect, almost reverence, for Catholicism. He told me once of an experience he had at Notre Dame. He was with Father Theodore Hesburgh, president of Notre Dame, shortly before delivering a speech there. Their meeting was interrupted by a young priest who had just been a witness to what turned out to be a fatal traffic accident. He had stopped his car and asked if he could be of any help. "Yes, Father," a policeman said. "This man is dying and says he is a Catholic. Can you give him extreme unction?" The priest rushed over to the dying man, knelt by him, and performed the last rites. "Isn't that wonderful," Father Hesburgh replied, a beatific look on his face. "Because you were there, this man is now with his Father in heaven."

My father told this story with a deep sense of reverence and awe. He could not believe. But he believed in belief. Nominally, he listed himself as a Presbyterian. I think that he did this for my mother. Shortly before he died, she asked him, however, if he would like to see a priest. He said no. Yet his last significant conversation was with a deeply devout Catholic cousin, John Church. As I look back on it, I think perhaps that John served as my father's priest in his last hours.

As for myself, I was raised a Presbyterian, but it never really took. In fact, my interest in religion was purely academic until the combination of Thomas Jefferson, George Williams, Rhys Williams, First and Second Church, and Harvard began to filter into my soul.

In large part, I base my faith upon the teachings of Jesus. As dramatically as anyone in history, Jesus lived in such a way that his life proved to have been worth dying for. And yet, from the Apostles' Creed, embraced as doctrine throughout much of Christendom, one would have little way of telling this. It says that he was born in an unusual way and died in an unusual way, but tells us nothing about the fact that Jesus *lived* in an unusual way. To me it is precisely this that is most important about Jesus. Not that he existed before he was born; not that he was implanted in a virgin's womb; not that he visited hell after he died; and not that he returned to be resurrected and to reign in heaven. These are dogmatic propositions of faith. They can be confirmed by faith alone, and a mighty leap of faith at that, for they stand in direct contradiction of what we know of nature's laws. What is truly important about Jesus is how he lived. It is the power of his love, the penetrating simplicity of his teachings, the force of his example of service on behalf of the disenfranchised and downtrodden. It is the witness of his life itself that speaks so eloquently to our human condition.

For us, who were born in the usual way and shall die in the usual way, it is Jesus' unusual life here on earth that really matters. For we too are called to lead unusual lives, evincing in our deeds testimony to our innate potential for goodness and righteousness and love. The Apostles' Creed and other such statements of dogmatic theology seem to miss this point entirely. They seem to say, "If you believe in Jesus, you can live forever," not "If you believe like Jesus, you can live well."

Over time, I had come to revere my father for one reason above all others, and that was his integrity. He matched word with deed as well as any person I have ever known. This same challenge is what drew me finally to the Unitarian ministry. In the ceremony with which we welcome new members to All Souls, each individual is charged henceforth to reject those beliefs she finds to be false and to embrace those she discovers to be true. The same principle holds for a Unitarian Universalist minister. I am charged to say what I believe, nothing more and nothing less. This may not seem like much, but how many of us manage to do this even in our daily lives, not to mention in our houses of worship?

Amy and I had several friends at divinity school who were ordained as Episcopalian or Presbyterian ministers who were openly scornful of such things as the Apostles' Creed and even of the trinity. They had convinced themselves that these things didn't really matter, for the true test of religion is in how one lives one's life. I agree with this latter statement, but I also feel that it does matter that we believe the words we speak, especially in church.

My own minister in Manhattan—ministers too need ministers—is an Episcopalian clergyman, Hays Rockwell, the rector of St. James. The reason I feel so at home with Hays is not that we believe the same things, for we do not. I feel at home with him because we both believe what we say, and because we respect one another's convictions, however different.

I don't mean to suggest that I entered the Unitarian Universalist ministry for the same reason that my father entered the United States Senate. It is just that, given my father's example, one thing above all others mattered to me and that was honesty. I independently chose to devote my life to religion. Having made this decision, however, I could not play games, either with myself or with God.

I was called to serve All Souls as its minister in early February of 1978. My father was gratified, I think, not for theological but for practical reasons. He saw it as a step in the right direction. "Well, Forrest," he said. "Out of the ivory tower and into the real world."

One hurdle remained. I still had to finish my dissertation. I did this by disappearing into the bowels of the Harvard Andover Library for four months. During this

time, I had little idea what was going on in the outside
world. One of the things that was going on was a pitched
battle on the floor of the U.S. Senate over the Panama
Canal Treaties.

In early 1978, the Carter administration signed an
agreement—one that had been sought by three U.S.
presidents—to turn control of the Panama Canal over to
the Republic of Panama by the end of the century. Frank
Church was the ranking Democrat on the Senate Foreign Relations Committee. The committee's chairman,
Senator John Sparkman of Alabama, was in failing
health and not able to present a vigorous case for the
treaties' ratification on the Senate floor. Though he knew
that the treaties were bitterly opposed by a large majority of the people of Idaho, Frank Church took on the
task.

At the height of the debate over the treaties' ratification, in a major floor address, he explained his position
on this issue in terms of his overall philosophy concerning the U.S. role in the developing world. The theme he
struck recurs again and again in his writings, finally to
be stated most completely in the last article Church
would ever write just a month before he died. In April
of 1978, he put it this way: "We have known since 1964
that the time of reckoning would come, that the United
States could not preserve a colony in a world where
colonies have disappeared; that in the end, we would
have to acknowledge to Panama what we claimed for
ourselves from the days of Lexington and Concord—the
right of our own independence and sovereign control
over our own land."

Frank Church's work as floor manager for ratification
of the Panama Canal Treaties was an important mile-
stone in his Senate career. It also contributed to his defeat for reelection in 1980. During a newspaper interview
in April 1979, Church admitted, "The Panama Canal

Treaties were not popular anywhere and I knew it would cost votes." Undoubtedly it did. As it turned out, however, the Panama Canal Treaties were not the determining factor in Church's defeat in 1980. Jimmy Carter was.

During the last four years of Frank Church's twenty-four-year service in the Senate, Jimmy Carter was President. During the last two years of Jimmy Carter's presidency, Frank Church was chairman of the Foreign Relations Committee. Throughout, their relationship was rigidly impersonal and strained.

Frank Church could have been very helpful to Jimmy Carter. That he was not is due in large measure to an almost complete lack of communication between the two of them, even at critical moments when Church's counsel and support might have proved valuable. Part of the problem had to do with Carter's congressional relations in general. Little effort was made to cultivate even the most senior members of Congress. When efforts were finally made, they were often bungled. Beyond this, Carter himself, having run against the establishment, was disinclined to curry favor within it. Church could understand. He, too, had little use for the old boy network. But he had even less sympathy for the good old boy network that Carter had erected in its place.

One incident in particular is emblematic of the awkwardness of Carter's relations with congressional leaders. It was at a time when increasing displeasure was being voiced both in Congress and in the Washington press over Carter's aloofness. Church received a call one morning from the White House. Would he and Bethine like to join two other senators and their wives that night for a relaxing evening with the Carters? Church readily accepted. He called Bethine. She drove to the Senate with a change of clothing for him, and after the last vote of the day, at eight o'clock the two of them arrived at the White House.

To begin with, not only they but all of the guests were conspicuously overdressed for the occasion. President and Mrs. Carter, outfitted casually in slacks and sweaters, came in after everyone had arrived. My father later reported that it was the only time in his life when he was not wearing a tuxedo and still felt like a penguin. "Would you like to see a movie?" Carter asked. Naturally, they said that they would. Popcorn and Scotch was served, and for the next two hours the group sat in the White House screening room and watched a movie.

Two sandwiches were brought in by an aide. "Rosalynn and I haven't eaten," Carter said. "I hope you all won't mind if we two have our dinner while we all talk?" That no one else had eaten seemed not to have occurred to the Carters. So the senators and their wives talked and sat while the Carters ate their sandwiches. Church had hoped that he finally might be able to speak with Carter about pressing concerns in the Foreign Relations Committee. Instead, the entire "dinner" discussion centered on the movie they had just seen. At eleven o'clock, Carter retired for the evening and the three senators with whom he had hoped to become better acquainted were on their way home.

A contrasting story. Frank Church had a love affair with the people of Israel. Of all the world leaders he had known, none impressed him quite as much as Golda Meir. Church was fond of telling one story in particular about her. In 1969, he and Simcha Dinitz, later Israel's ambassador to the United States, were visiting the prime minister in her home. When they sat down, she asked them whether they would like sandwiches and tea. They were pleased to accept, and she disappeared into the kitchen.

After about five minutes, overcome with curiosity, Church got up to see what the prime minister was doing. He cracked the door to the kitchen and peeked in. There was Golda Meir, wearing an apron, brewing the tea and preparing the sandwiches herself. Church was speechless. Golda Meir turned around and smiled at him. "Senator, I know why you are here. You have come into the kitchen to help. And that is very kind, but I am just about done. You go back and sit down, and I shall be right with you."

For the next two hours they spoke of international relations, of the Soviet Union, and most intensely, about the long-term prospects for peace in the Middle East. As Church was leaving, the last thing that Prime Minister Meir said to him was, "Senator, next time when you come I will bake you a nice little cake. I just didn't have time to this morning, but next time I promise you I will."

Compared to his chairmanship of the Multinationals Subcommittee and the Intelligence Committee, Church's term as chairman of the Foreign Relations Committee was not particularly distinguished. For one thing, the chairman's position had declined in influence from the days of William Borah and even of William Fulbright. During Senator John Sparkman's tenure, more ambitious and capable senators took advantage of his relatively weak leadership to divide the committee and its staff into little fiefdoms for themselves. When Church took over, he attempted to reverse this by eliminating subcommittees. This angered several of his colleagues and led to friction within the staff. Moreover, seniority was no longer the guarantee of authority that it had been when Church first came to the Senate twenty-two years before. Church's attempt to assume control of the committee was not only resented but actively contested by several junior members. Having waited so long for the fulfillment of his boyhood dream, he could not help but be a bit disappointed in the way that it came true. Moreover, by the time he got things running in the way he wanted them to, Church had other things on his mind. He was locked in a desperate battle for political survival back home in Idaho.

Two independent committees had been formed to raise money to unseat Frank Church. The Committee for Positive Change and the Anyone But Church Committee were both active by the summer of 1979, running ads in Idaho. One was filmed next to an empty Titan missile silo just outside of Mountain Home. The charge was that Church's opposition to military appropriations had shut the silo down, thus leaving Idaho defenseless against enemy attack. By this time, the Titan missile was obsolete. It had been replaced by the Minuteman, which Church had supported. Nonetheless, the charge, linked with Church's open opposition to the B-1 bomber, was beginning to have an impact on the Idaho electorate.

Church accused NCPAC, the parent organization for the Anyone But Church Committee, of utilizing the Hitler "big lie" technique. As reported in the Washington *Post* on August 10, 1980, Terry Dolan, the head of NCPAC, was to boast, "A group like ours could lie through its teeth and the candidate it helps stays clean." On another occasion that June, the Miami *Herald* attributed to Dolan that "through effective use of propaganda, . . . NCPAC could elect Mickey Mouse."

Church was running scared in Idaho. He returned in August of 1979 to combat the charges being made against him. In addition to the Panama Canal Treaties and the claim that he was weak on defense, another issue being cited as evidence that Church was "soft on communism" was Church's meeting with Fidel Castro on a recent visit to Cuba.

In August of 1977, Frank and Bethine had spent three full days with Fidel Castro in Cuba. While they were there, Church also negotiated on behalf of people with American passports who had been unable to leave Cuba since the revolution because they could not take their families with them. He won a small diplomatic coup when Castro agreed that eighty-seven of them were now free to take their families and return home to the United States.

It was a stunning trip. Fidel Castro took Frank and Bethine on a tiring but fascinating whirlwind two-day tour of Cuba. With Fidel himself at the wheel of a Soviet-made jeep, together they visited cooperative farms, model housing projects, and even a rum distillery. They also went spearfishing at the Bay of Pigs, where CIA-backed anti-Castro exiles had attempted to invade the island in 1961.

My father told me later how strange it was swimming underwater with Castro, the two of them armed with spear guns. Just a few years before it had been Church himself who uncovered the bizarre CIA plots against Castro's life. He looked in a different way than he otherwise might have at the seashells and the wet suits, even at the cigars that they smoked after their swim. Each had been a designated instrument of murder.

Every day, my parents and Castro talked late into the evening. Castro wanted to know all about Idaho, its agriculture and mining industry, big-game hunting and fishing, how high the mountains were. They also spoke openly of Cuban military intervention in Africa, and the possibility of trade with the United States. It had long been my father's view that we forced Castro to a position of complete dependency upon the Soviet Union by our trade embargo. Furthermore, he did not understand how we could recognize and trade with the Soviet Union, while at the same time refusing to recognize and trade with Cuba. It made neither political nor practical sense.

Before returning to the United States, Church and Castro held a press conference at the Havana Airport. Castro made his concessions, thus ensuring the success of Church's trip. Church thanked Castro and expressed the belief that they had become personal friends. Castro in turn praised Church as an "important, courageous politician" who was "capable, serious and intellectual . . . a man you can talk to." A picture of the two of them together with appropriate quotes attached was the centerpiece of a major NCPAC tract distributed broadly throughout Idaho in July 1979.

That August, preoccupation with both Cuba and his electoral troubles was to lead to the most lamentable episode of Frank Church's Senate career. On August 30, just before his return to Washington after a month of campaigning, Church received a call from Under Secretary of State David Newsom, informing him that U.S. intelligence had discovered Soviet troops in Cuba and that the information would soon "surface." One problem with this was that as recently as a month before, reports of a possible Soviet troop presence in Cuba had been denied by the CIA in a meeting of the Foreign Relations Committee. For Church it was almost déjà vu, recalling the final days of his 1962 reelection campaign. The problem now was that Senator Stone of Florida, who had been pressing this issue, would surely be irate, and possibly be joined by several Republicans on the committee in an effort to establish linkage between this and the impending Senate ratification of the Salt II Treaty.

Church called Secretary Cyrus Vance and asked what they were planning to do. Vance indicated that, rather than making an announcement or issue a protest, they would allow the information to leak. Given the probable reaction of Senator Stone and others on his committee, Church said that if the administration had no plans to make an announcement, he himself would. Vance told Church that he was free to do so. After repeated efforts to reach President Carter in Plains were unsuccessful,

Church decided to issue a press release outlining the new information and condemning the Soviet presence in Cuba.

Here is where Church made his first mistake. This was a major news opportunity, and his press secretary thought that if he was going to do anything, he might as well go for major exposure, especially given his vulnerability in Idaho on the Cuba issue. So they decided to grandstand. Instead of issuing a statement, Church called a televised press conference that evening in his home in Boise.

From that point on, he was swept by the tide of events. For one thing, while he had initially held that the Salt II Treaty should stand or fall on its own merits, he soon discovered the impracticality of this view. Perhaps looking for an excuse upon which to defend their opposition to the treaty, several members of the Foreign Relations Committee indicated that they would not vote to send it to the floor unless the Soviets removed their combat troops from Cuba. Then, on September 5, the same day he was scheduled to appear before the Senate Foreign Relations Committee, Secretary Vance held a news conference in which he identified the troops for the first time as a "brigade." When asked whether he would ask the Soviets to remove the brigade, he answered, "I will not be satisfied with the maintenance of the status quo." By September 6, Church admitted that "there is no likelihood whatever the Senate would ratify the SALT Treaty as long as Russian combat troops remain stationed in Cuba."

Now Church was backed into a corner. Had he not taken the leadership on this issue in the first place, he would not have been obliged to continue pressing what was becoming increasingly more trivial yet more nettlesome a problem. The CIA admitted that in going over their records carefully the combat troops had been in

Cuba for years and were not a new brigade. In addition, unlike the missiles in 1962, they posed no real threat to the United States. What they posed a threat to was the SALT Treaty, something for which Church had fought long and hard. No matter who had made the announcement of the troops' presence in Cuba, even if it had been leaked to the press, Church was surely right in his assessment that SALT II would be linked to this issue. The problem was that Church was identified, uncharacteristically, among the belligerents. He did fashion language in an amendment which made it possible to get the treaty out of committee and onto the floor. But shortly thereafter, the Soviets invaded Afghanistan, Americans were held hostage in Iran, and Carter himself withdrew the treaty in protest.

Later my father told me that even though he felt scapegoated by the White House and trapped by the antitreaty forces, he had erred badly by seizing this issue in the way that he had. The main problem was that it was so uncharacteristic of him. One of his Democratic colleagues quipped that Church "was like Robert Redford trying to play John Wayne—woefully out of character."

As it turned out the brigade issue had no bearing on the outcome of the 1980 election. It did tarnish Church's credentials, however, as one politician who followed his conscience and not the blowing wind.

In Idaho, Congressman Steven Symms, a hard-line right-wing Republican, announced for Frank Church's seat in the Senate. Symms is an affable man, unpretentious in manner. I have always liked him. He is, however, neither particularly quick on his feet, nor effective as a legislator. In his eight years in Congress, he did not author a single piece of legislation. But the people of Idaho were shy of big government. Symms ran against Washington, even as Ronald Reagan did. His ineffectiveness as a congressman was not a liability in Idaho.

It was a remarkable campaign. Church and Symms spent almost $2 million apiece. Despite the outcome, it was the most effective race Church ever ran. Early on, NCPAC became a liability for Symms. Despite the vaunting claims by Terry Dolan, this was one race where his efforts almost cost his candidate the election. Though they spent a quarter of a million dollars in Idaho, more than they invested in any other race, by October their efforts began to backfire. Church hammered hard against the negative campaigning and pulled nine points ahead of Symms in the last published poll, which reflected our own sounding of how the election was going two weeks before election day.

Amy and Twig and I spent August in Idaho. Again, we were out on the campaign trail. I remember in particular one two-week road swing. Twig was almost two years old—old enough to be featured on one of his grandfather's commercials, but not old enough to keep from getting carsick on windy Idaho roads. We appeared in parades. Our presence was announced at rodeos. We visited local papers and county fairs. In one small town we all got food poisoning at the better of the two local restaurants.

One of the reasons that the campaign was so sustaining was that it was run by best friends. Carl Burke, my father's old soul mate from Boise High and Stanford, the manager of his presidential campaign and all his other four races for the Senate, was again campaign manager. And Peter Fenn, my best friend since ninth grade, whom my mother calls her third son, was my father's administrative assistant, the highest staff position in a senator's office.

I once commented to Peter how amazing it all was: he, scion of an old Massachusetts family, the grandson of a Unitarian minister and great-grandson of a former dean of the Harvard Divinity School, and I, the son of a

United States senator from Idaho, had traded places. I had attended Harvard Divinity School and was now a Unitarian minister in New York City. He was in Idaho as the head of my father's staff.

I am not sure how many true friends one person can have during a lifetime—perhaps no more than three or four. As the campaign rolled on, I thought of Peter and me, and compared our friendship to that of my father and Carl. Next to my parents, my wife, and my children, never have I loved anyone more. And the same was true with Dad and Carl. They cared about the same things. They deeply believed that every single person can make a profound difference. And they had the same infectious sense of humor. What hair Carl had left he let down in my father's company. The two of them talked still as if they were in high school plotting the country's future. The only difference was that now they really were.

I returned to Boise from New York four days before the election. There was a general, if cautious, level of optimism in the air. But my father said to me the night that I arrived, "Don't get your hopes up. It looks to me as if Carter is going to crash this weekend. If he does, we might go down with him."

The news that weekend focused on Iran. On Monday, the word broke. "Iran OKs hostage-release terms." All it did was to remind people of how long both the country and the President had been held hostage. Furthermore, there was cynicism everywhere. "Why now?"

The final weekend, pro-lifers put tens of thousands of one-page leaflets onto the windshields of cars in church lots and adjacent streets all over the state. Despite the claims of the new religious right, it likely had little effect on the outcome. What really happened that weekend is that the Carter campaign completely collapsed, not only in Idaho but all across the country.

The largest paper in the state, the *Idaho Statesman*,

endorsed Reagan and Church. "One measure of a U.S. senator is whether he takes stands that are later proven right by history. History has treated Church well," the editorial read. Many people in Idaho agreed with both of the *Statesman*'s endorsements. Jimmy Carter received 26 percent of the vote in Idaho. Church lost by just a little over 4,000 votes, 218,701 to 214,439.

For years Frank Church defied conventional political wisdom. As an outspoken liberal, he represented a conservative western state in the U.S. Senate for twenty-four years. On the day of his defeat, Rod Gramer of the *Idaho Statesman* accounted for Church's defeat as follows. "Four factors probably led to Church's defeat: the state of the nation's economy; his support for the Panama Canal Treaties; the 11th-hour blitz by right-wing groups; and, perhaps most importantly, the coattails of Ronald Reagan. . . . In a race as close as the one between Symms and Church, Reagan's coattails made all the difference in the world."

There was one more thing. Carter conceded his election two hours before the polls were closed in Democratic northern Idaho, which falls within the Pacific time zone. Pollster Peter Hart later used Church's race as a demonstration of the way in which Carter's early concession affected outcomes in the west. I am not sure that it made the final difference, but turnout was lower in the north and many of our pollwatchers saw people turn around in the parking lots rather than cast their ballots during the final two hours when the election booths were open.

Terry Dolan, NCPAC, and various other right-wing religious groups can claim a degree of credit in several Senate races in 1980. George McGovern, Birch Bayh, and Dick Clark all lost by more than 10 percent of the vote. Church, however, despite the fact that Idaho gave Reagan a greater majority than any state save neighboring

Utah, came within less than half a single percentage point of keeping his seat.

Throughout the evening of his defeat, Frank and Bethine remained chipper. They took it upon themselves to lighten the atmosphere, telling stories, cracking jokes. I cried that night. My parents did not.

The next morning the family gathered on the lawn of the Clark home in Boise, and Frank Church was met with a huge contingent of national and local press. The first question was, "Senator, what are you and Bethine going to do now?" He laughed, put his arm around my mother, and said, "I think we'll stay together."

My parents were best friends as well as sweethearts for more than forty years. They were a political team, both on the campaign trail and in Washington. They were consistently called one of the happiest couples in Washington. When asked about the secret to their successful marriage, Bethine replied, "Oh, my husband and I never run out of interesting conversation."

A good marriage is harder to describe than a bad one. As Bethine once told a reporter, "I find it so hard to talk about our marriage except positively. It comes off a little like those sunsets they paint on calendars." When asked about her unofficial title as "Idaho's third senator," she freely would admit to viewing their life together as a joint career, but then balk at how this might sound.

In her book *The Power Lovers*, Myra MacPherson described Frank and Bethine as "a most happy team couple," something admitted to even by "the most cynical examiners of the public happy-family mask worn by unhappy political families." She goes on to say, "An interview with them comes dangerously close to sounding like a parody of those *Modern Screen* stories about Hollywood's rare phenomenon, the long-standing happily wed duo. Gossip swirls around Washington couples like autumn leaves circling in the wind, but not around the

Churches. When I mentioned to people that I was trying to find some political couples who had successfully worked out a balance between their public and private life, the first answer was always, 'Have you talked to Frank and Bethine Church?' "

Frank Church would readily admit that Bethine was the greatest influence in his life. "She's aware of all the pressures," he told Myra MacPherson. "Probably one reason we have a happy marriage is that she understands all of politics . . . Politics is an insecure profession. The people who choose it are driven to it—that's not true of their wives."

Of the two, Bethine was the better campaigner. I can remember sitting with my family having breakfast in a tiny road café. My father was really quite shy. He was uncomfortable forcing himself on others. "Frank, that couple over there in the corner. They want to meet you."

"Bethy," he would say, "they are having their breakfast."

"Just go over and say, 'Hi.' " And so he would.

My father and mother's marriage was not all sweetness and light, but it was never less than lively. Bethine described herself once as "combustible . . . a worrier who laughs a lot." As to their relationship, in an interview published in the Boston *Globe* shortly before he ran for President, Bethine said, "Power is a scary commodity. It's so easily mischanneled. Well, I'm the burr under my husband's saddle. Often I appoint myself his Personal Leveler. I remind him who we are, where we're going, and how we're getting there. Actually, I take a little whack at him. Then we have a great big laugh together.

"Sometimes, I can get into a towering rage. In our married life, I've been known to throw a few things around. You'd be surprised how quickly that can clear the air. When we were first married, some people said that Frank and I were so much alike we'd either get along or clash like the dickens. It's been a lot of the former and a little of the latter.

"Of course the secret is knowing how to control one's temper and laughing a lot. My pop taught me that this world was made for a lot of crying and you have to master the art of laughing to make up for all the tears."

Shortly after his defeat, Frank Church joined the New York law firm Whitman and Ransom. He worked out of their Washington office, specializing in international law. His arrangement with Whitman and Ransom allowed him extensive freedom to write and lecture around the country on foreign and domestic policy.

One thing about his retirement delighted Frank Church. He was unabashed in his pleasure at making money. Frank and Bethine had scraped to get by for twenty-four years in the U.S. Senate. The cost of maintaining two houses on a Senate salary made each year a struggle just to stay even. In 1964, one-third of the way through his Senate career, in disclosing his financial statement, Frank Church admitted that the $15,000 he had had in the bank and in municipal bonds when he entered the Senate had been cut in half. In fact, I can remember when I first visited his Senate office, I asked my mother, "Why is it that Daddy is so rich, while we are so poor?"

Things did not measurably improve over the next twenty-four years. Within a year of being retired from the Senate, Church, from his law practice and lectures, was earning four times as much money as he ever had before.

Church was fond of telling the story of his visit on a fact-finding mission to Hawaii, when Congress was debating statehood for the islands. He met then with representatives from several wealthy families whose forebears had first come to Hawaii as missionaries. They told him that their ancestors had come there to "do good." Now, more than a century later, they—the descendants—were doing "very well." In a meeting with a group of Idaho Democrats in 1983, Church made the same observation about himself. "In 1957 I went to the U.S. Senate to do good. Now I am doing very well."

During the final four years of his life, Church traveled widely throughout the world, both on legal business and as a speaker. He and Bethine visited Denmark, West Germany, France, Italy, Yugoslavia, Israel, Lebanon, Australia, New Zealand, Taiwan, the People's Republic of China, South Korea, Japan, Canada, and Panama— many of these countries more than once.

Wherever he went, he met with foreign leaders. "No one overseas understands our political system," my father told me. "They greet me as a member of the shadow government, waiting in the wings for the next election."

Two of the last public appearances Frank Church was to make characterized his strong antiestablishment bias when it came to the shaping of American foreign policy. The first occasion was in October 1983, when he delivered the keynote address for Russian Awareness Week in Boise, Idaho. On that occasion, as he had so many times before, Church said that the United States was more threatened by the nuclear arms race than by Soviet imperialism and Communist aggression. "Today our homeland is subject to destruction in the next thirty minutes. That is the bottom line on all the hundreds of billions spent, all the blood spilled in foreign wars, all the anguish and waste. Today the security of our whole people is more palpably at risk than ever before."

There is another quote from that same speech that touches me deeply. My mother, brother, and I are putting it on my father's tombstone: "Every citizen who loves this country, its freedom and good life; every parent whose children yearn for their day in the sun; every American who believes our national heritage still represents 'the last, best hope on earth,' must become earnestly engaged in the active quest for peace."

The second occasion was on November 29, 1983, when Church debated Zbigniew Brzezinski at the Center for National Policy in Washington on "The Uses and Limits of U.S. Power," with specific reference to American intervention in Grenada.

"For those who believe that the sword is swift and sure, Grenada is proof positive," Church said. "The island is made to order for quick and easy conquest by the United States. . . . But Ronald Reagan's triumph in Grenada yielded even more impressive results at home, where the Democratic Party was put to rout, and the President's popularity jumped ten percentage points. Never mind that the invasion violated international law and our solemn pledges under the charters of the United Nations and the Organization of American States; never mind that it was condemned by a vote of 108 to 9 in the U.N. General Assembly; never mind that the press was censored and the American people spoon-fed their information by the Pentagon, acting for the first time as a ministry of propaganda; never mind that rescuing the students, if ever they were in danger, didn't require a military seizure of the entire island and the dismantling of its government; America finally won a clear-cut victory no matter how small. President Reagan cowed the Democrats by nailing a little Marxist pelt on the White House wall."

One of the things my father enjoyed most during his last years was the time he spent with his grandchildren. What truly delighted him was that, against all odds, Amy and I finally brought a girl into the Church family in March of 1981.

Nina Wynne Church is her grandfather's girl. As a matter of fact, if there is to be another politician in the Church family, it is likely to be Nina. She is outgoing, thick-skinned, unabashed, appealingly verbal, and almost always in charge. Nina and my father hit it off brilliantly. They understood one another. Nina's devotion to her grandfather even in the last difficult weeks was complete. Not liking to be separated from him, she vowed to "keep him company" even during potentially daunting blood tests and injections. "Opa's brave," she said. "Opa doesn't cry when he bleeds. I'm brave too."

Nina and Twig were blessed with an ample amount of their grandfather's time, far more than would have been the case had he still been in the Senate. One or two weeks a year my parents would take the children, while Amy and I stole away for a bit of vacation time alone. They and Chase would take them to the little cabin on Friends Creek in Pennsylvania that my parents purchased after his defeat in 1980. My father said to me before he died that he had only two regrets, that he would not be able to see his grandchildren grow up, and that he and my mother would not grow old together.

I think my father enjoyed my small successes at All Souls. Within six years, the congregation had more than doubled in size and attendance. He and my mother visited us often. I have since learned that inwardly he cringed at some of my sermons, confiding to my mother that if I ever did decide to run for public office, my opponent would only have to rummage through the All Souls archives for a whole campaign's worth of ammunition. Also, my father never could quite accommodate himself to New York City. He relished referring to Amy's and my apartment as a "luxury tenement."

My father and I spent very little time discussing religion. I am not sure why. In part, he did not understand my passion for it. He measured things in terms of impact. Mine was not great.

There were a few whimsical moments in our interchange on the subject of religion. I can remember two in

particular. The occasion of each was a prayer. In 1976 my
father came to Massachusetts to explore the possibility of
entering the Democratic primary. We had dinner at the
Union Club. Among those present was John Kerry,
elected in 1984 to the Senate from Massachusetts. I was
asked to give the blessing. Having just been ordained, I
had never performed in this manner before. So I invited
everyone around the table to hold hands and join together in a "Quaker" blessing. A minute of silence
passed and I said, "Amen." To which my father replied,
"That, son, is a copout."

A year later we were together in North Carolina,
where my father, at the invitation of Governor James B.
Hunt, was combining a speech and a family vacation. We
went to a "pig picking." The term is descriptive. There
were about a hundred people standing in a long driveway waiting to eat a pig. I was asked to "offer thanks."
They led me to the porch above. Silence fell. Echoing a
favorite prayer of Krister Stendahl, my dean at Harvard,
I invoked the divine blessing by saying, "Dear God, for
those in this world who hunger give them food, and for
those of us with food in abundance, give us a hunger
for righteousness." I forgot to say amen. There was a
certain amount of confusion. For one thing, the prayer
was too short. Most of all it was foreign. My father said
afterwards, "You blew your prayer, son. You should
have said, 'For thems of us who's got pig, let's eat pig—
for thems that don't, let 'em eat cake.' "

We did have a conversation about religion and my
calling shortly before my father died. He was concerned
that the power of religion was being co-opted by the
religious right. Once he even went so far as to call Nor-
man Lear, telling him to look me up as someone who
might be able to provide an alternative to the electronic
evangelists. Lear did call. I sent him the only video tape
I had of myself preaching. Our church has no video

equipment so I never saw it myself. In any event, Lear never called back.

What my father told me before he died was that we have very little time left on this planet. He charged me to do whatever I could to make a difference. It was a hard challenge. For one thing, I am not sure what that might be. I am now thirty-six years old. At that age Frank Church was nearing the end of his first term in the U.S. Senate. I told him that I would do everything I could. It might not be equal to what he had done, but I would do my best.

My father's defeat in 1980 was not a tragedy. One reason for this is that neither he nor my mother believed in unhappy endings. So when Frank Church was defeated for the Senate, the two of them sat down and enumerated all the advantages of private life. As it turned out, because of the luxury of time they would have to spend together, the last three years of his life were in many ways their happiest. "Maybe people are like geraniums," Frank Church said in an April 1983 interview. "Maybe it is best that they are uprooted once in a while and replanted in different soil."

6. Saying Good-bye

Of all the things I am called upon to do as a minister, none is more important, and none has proved of greater value to me, than the call to be with people at times of loss. I would almost go so far as to say that I did not become a minister until I performed my first funeral. When asked at a recent gathering of colleagues what gives most meaning to my work, I replied that, above all else, it is the constant reminder of death. Death awakens me to life's preciousness and also its fragility.

How often this happens. My desk and mind may be littered with a hundred tasks and grievances, things to begrudge life about. Then death or the threat of dying comes calling at my door. All of a sudden, like a bracing wind, it clears my being of all pettiness. It awakens me to the precariousness of life and the wonder of love. It brings me a renewed perspective upon life's real joy and real pain. What a blessing this is, not death but life, fully felt, demanding all my human resources. This is death's hard gift to me. It not only justifies my work, but makes me whole again.

In large measure, this is what my calling is about—a

human response to the dual reality of being alive and having to die. Regardless of faith or creed, in this we are all companions. The word *companion* goes back to the Latin root "con," meaning with, and "pan" meaning bread. A companion is one with whom we break bread. In a spiritual rather than material sense, the ultimate bread we mortals break together is the bread of life and death.

Amy and I learned that my father was seriously ill shortly before Christmas of 1983. He was losing weight and strength rapidly. We felt it might have something to do with a diabetic condition that was diagnosed shortly after he left the Senate. He and his doctor had never got his sugar levels under control.

My parents and Chase had intended to spend Christmas in New York with us. Amy's family would be there. Her father and mother, Gordon and Nina Furth, were coming from Papua New Guinea, where Gordon, as president of a subsidiary of Standard of Indiana, was overseeing the progress of the Ok Tedi mine. Amy's sister, Wynne, a lawyer in Claremont, California, and her brother-in-law, Don Brenneis, a professor at Pitzer College, were bringing their daughter, Val, to complete the family circle. For the first time in years, it was to be a full family celebration.

During the week before Christmas, my father went through a series of extensive but inconclusive tests. His condition was worsening, though the doctors could not determine the cause. When it became apparent that my father would not be able to travel, Amy and I immediately flew to Washington, where we found him weak but in good spirits. We returned to New York just in time for Christmas Eve and Christmas Day services at All Souls. It was to be the first of more than a dozen such trips over the next three months.

There were close to a thousand people at church on

Christmas Eve. "To celebrate the birth of Jesus is to affirm life's sacred potential by attesting to the power of love to remake humankind," I told them. "With his birth we may each, in a way, be born again, renewed in that love which alone can save our world and give meaning to our lives."

I was thinking of my father. I was thinking of the gift he had given me nearly thirty years before, Thomas Jefferson's Bible, and of Jefferson's definition of religion: "It is in our deeds and not in our words that our religion must be read."

I returned to Washington with Twig on Christmas Day and again with Nina for New Year's Eve. My father was gaunt and jaundiced. I think that he knew he was dying. The immediate frustration, however, was in not knowing why. Shortly after New Year's we made arrangements for him to fly to Memorial Sloan-Kettering Cancer Center in New York for diagnostic tests and a surgical procedure to unblock his bile duct.

The people at Sloan-Kettering were wonderful, as were my parents' friends in New York. Henry Kimelman, Bill and Bubbles Landau, and Ambassador Warren Manshel and his wife, Anita, were with them constantly. Mother stayed with Don and Marian Burros. She spent twelve hours every day at the hospital, and then, often, would go to some odd corner of New York City and have dinner with Marian, food critic for *The New York Times*.

Church's Senate colleagues were particularly solicitous. Ted Kennedy was the first to call. Kennedy then got on the phone and located George McGovern, who was campaigning in Iowa. George was in touch throughout my father's illness. Senator Alan Simpson, Republican from Wyoming, visited my father in the hospital. He had been riding in a cab, and the driver asked him what he did. "I am a U.S. senator," Simpson replied.

"Then you must know Frank Church."

"Of course I know Frank."

"Frank Church is the one politician I really admire," the cabbie replied. "Did you know that he was in the hospital here?" Simpson had not known, but upon learning this he asked the driver to take him there. My parents were deeply moved, both by his story and by his visit.

The last call Church received on the evening before his surgery was from Steven Symms, the man who had unseated him in 1980. "I just want to tell you, Frank, that the last three years have been the greatest of my life," he said in closing. "I really love the Senate." Symms's call was well-meaning I am sure, but my mother was furious. My father was amused.

Before he went in for surgery, Church wrote greetings to Mayor Andrew Young, whom he was scheduled to introduce as principal speaker at the annual Frank Church Conference on Public Affairs sponsored by Boise State University. He apologized for not being there in person. "Instead, I find myself in the hospital playing matador against a bull who has me at a distinct disadvantage." Citing Young's close association with Dr. Martin Luther King, Jr., in the struggle for civil rights, Church concluded his in absentia introduction by saying, "That struggle continues today, and, therefore, it is especially appropriate that this conference is devoted to the subject of political repression and social control in this Orwellian year of 1984."

On January 12, Frank Church was operated on. They performed the bile duct bypass procedure, but discovered an inoperable malignant tumor on the pancreas. The cancer had spread to Church's liver, and there was no hope for recovery.

Three days later I was scheduled to preach a sermon commemorating Martin Luther King's birthday. I spoke instead about my father. "As many of you know, my father is seriously ill," I said. "In light of this, I know you will forgive me for changing my sermon topic. This morning, I need to grapple once again, in new ways and old, with love and death."

I spoke of my father's bout with cancer thirty-five years before. "Ever since my father's illness and recovery, my parents have lived on borrowed time," I told my congregation. "Fully aware of life's fragility, they have not been afraid to risk and give of themselves fully. Life for them is not a given, but a gift. It is a gift with a price attached. That price is death. I am sure that they are still afraid of death. Few of us are not. Death is the ultimate mystery. But there is a way to counter this fear. We can live in such a way that our lives will prove to be worth dying for."

I had received a call two days before from Ari Goldman, a reporter for *The New York Times*. He wanted to interview me about how I was coping with my father's illness. Instead, I invited him to the service. Goldman wrote a sensitive story that appeared in the next morning's *Times*.

"Before the service," Goldman wrote, "Dr. Church stood on the steps of the Federal-style church building at 80th Street and Lexington Avenue and greeted his congregants with two-handed handshakes, kisses on the cheek and warm embraces. As they stood together momentarily in the morning cold, the congregants asked their minister, 'How is your father?'

" 'In good spirits.'

" 'What is the outlook for his recovery?' one asked.

" 'Not good.'

"But the 75-minute religious service had none of the gloom of the prognosis," Goldman went on to say. I am deeply grateful for that. It proved true of my father's funeral and memorial services as well. At All Souls this service on a winter's Sunday morning included a spir-

157

ited "Coronation March" by William Walton and "Sing God a Simple Song" by Leonard Bernstein. Coincidentally, almost a year to the day later, Bernstein himself preached at All Souls. That same month, January of 1985, George McGovern and Dr. Lewis Thomas, past head of Sloan-Kettering, also filled the pulpit. Their subject was "Hope in the Nuclear Age."

In my sermon I recalled a letter written by my mother to Natalie Davis Spingarn, quoted in Spingarn's book on living with cancer entitled, *Hanging in There: Living Well on Borrowed Time:* "Bethine Church wrote to me recently that I am quite right in feeling that the cancer twilight zone is a world that other people haven't lived in. Describing Senator Frank Church's fight with cancer thirty years ago, and their feeling that he then had only six months to live, she said that forever after he had been a different person. It had been somehow easier for him to do the things that needed to be done, and let the things that did not matter go."

I was reminded by this, and again during the period of my father's second battle with cancer, of how much my parents had taught me. Most of it had been taught by example and not by words. They never sat me down to inculcate the lessons that both of them had learned when my father was so very ill. They simply incorporated those lessons into the way they lived their lives. They possessed the courage to love, the courage to risk, the courage to lose, and they knew that the opposite of love is not hate, but fear.

This principle, a touchstone of my teacher, George Williams's, and of my father's own teachings, manifests itself in so many ways. For instance, we do not hate the Russians. We fear them. Fearing them, we imitate them and become more like them. We speak of windows of vulnerability. We arm ourselves to the teeth, rather than risking some accommodation that might lead to mutual cooperation and greater real security. My father knew this as well as anyone. It will take great courage to reduce our nuclear stockpiles, courage by both parties, because they fear us as much as we fear them.

"When Jesus said that we should love our enemies he was challenging us to risk our very lives for the sake of a higher truth," I told my congregation. "Such risk is redemptive simply because it changes our lives. Each of us will one day die. The question is, between now and then, how shall we choose to live?"

I thought of a second example. In New York, all of us are aware that beneath the shadows of our very houses there live hungry and homeless people. It is frightening even to contemplate. When I pass a shopping bag person on the street, I am tempted to avert my eyes, to walk on by and not let it register.

At our church we have a soup kitchen and also a hospitality and shelter program for homeless women. Everyone who has served in these programs has dared to risk an encounter with people whom before they had feared more than pitied. Such encounters are redemptive for all concerned. These people have begun to overcome their fear of us. We have begun to overcome our fear of them. In lowering our defenses in order to meet these people where they are, we have learned to live a little more fully the meaning of the second great commandment: "Thou shalt love thy neighbor as thyself."

Beyond this, there are so many instances in our daily lives when our fears stand in the way of our love. Every time we open ourselves up, every time we share ourselves with another, every time we commit ourselves to a cause or to a task that awaits our doing, we risk so much. We risk disappointment. We risk failure. We risk being rebuffed or being embarrassed or being inadequate. And beyond these things, we risk the enormous pain of loss.

"This morning we celebrate the birthday of a modern prophet and martyr, Martin Luther King, Jr.," I said. "His was a gospel of love—love answering hate, love overcoming fear and even death. He preached the kinship of all people, and witnessed to his faith by countering violence with nonviolence. He did not spend his life; he invested it in things that would ennoble and outlast him. His witness is a powerful beacon of hope that still illumines the public landscape in these dark and difficult times. Certainly Martin Luther King, Jr., lived in such a way that his life proved to be worth dying for. Especially when it came to love, he knew that the only things which are truly ours are those things we are prepared to give away.

"This, too, is the lesson that my parents taught me," I said in closing. "I keep forgetting it, of course. It is one of those lessons that one has to learn over and over again. It is one of those lessons that we learn by doing and forget by not doing. It is the lesson of love. Love thy enemy. Love thy neighbor as thyself. Cast out thy fear with love. And then—this I know—it will be somehow easier for us to do the things that need to be done, and to let the things that do not matter go."

After my sermon, I asked the congregation's indulgence one more time. I changed the final hymn from "The Battle Hymn of the Republic" to "Rank by Rank Again We Stand." Its closing verse is as follows:

Ours the years' memorial store,
Honored days and names we reckon,
Days of comrades gone before,
Lives that speak and deeds that beckon.
One in name, in honor one,
Guard we well the crown they won;
What they dreamed be ours to do,
Hope their hopes and seal them true.

160

Saying Good-bye

When I visited my father in the hospital on Monday, he had seen the *Times* article. We walked together down the hall and back. "Well, Forrest," he said to me, his eyes twinkling, "it looks like that is the last thing I'm going to be able to do to advance your career." To which he added, "It is a rare and somewhat mixed privilege to be able to read one's own eulogy in the morning paper."

My mother sat at the foot of my father's bed from eight o'clock in the morning to eight o'clock at night. Often she would read to him from the hundreds of letters and telegrams that were arriving daily from all over the country.

"Frank, listen to this one," she would say time and again.

Each letter was a gift to Frank and Bethine. Some brought tears of joy, others laughter. One man, who had never met Church, wrote to tell him about Vitamin E, which he contended had shrunk his dog's cancerous tumor. Church was sent sacred objects to put under his pillow and Bible verses to speed his recovery.

Steve Emerson, a former staff member, spent part of one day with Church in the hospital. He wrote of his experience in an article published January 22 in the *Idaho Statesman:*

> For ordinary men and women, the fear of cancer can destroy the ability to dream, to let the imagination run wild or to simply be curious. But there has been no lessening of Church's interest in life. He is as curious as ever. Despite a tiring and fatiguing day, he still was raring to go. . . . With the help of Bethine, he slowly twisted and slid out of bed and onto his feet. Within minutes, he was walking down the corridor, clasping and holding onto Bethine with one hand and pushing his intravenous stand with the other. He exchanged good cheer and humor as he encountered nurses, doctors and attendants during the trip. "What's the speed limit?" he asked one passer-by.

The hospital room was decorated with colorful paintings and drawings that Nina and Twig had made for their grandfather. Amy spent part of every afternoon playing backgammon with Frank. When my mother had finished the day's mail, she read to him from an espionage novel that Church had received for Christmas. He was fascinated by it.

Church flew home to Bethesda in a private jet on January 24. Over the next two and one-half months, in addition to a stream of visitors, both from Idaho and Washington, several of Church's closest friends, family members, and former staffers took turns living at the Church home to be with Frank and help Bethine. Carl Burke spent a week, as did Marilyn Burns, the daughter of his other closest high school friend. Family members Patsy Young and Beulah Reeves were there. George Kline, a beloved friend and staff member from his Idaho office, came to Bethesda for two weeks. And Church's brother, Dick, and his wife, Dicky, came almost every day. Of everyone, apart from Bethine, my brother, Chase, was probably the most helpful. Even at the very end, we did not have a nurse or attendant in the house, because Chase was always on call.

I visited my father almost every week, coming down to Washington on Sunday after church. One week I brought Twig with me, another week, Nina. Finally, Amy and I went together, leaving the children with friends in New York.

One of the things we talked about, often at great length, was my father's career and his political legacy. At first he was very insecure about it. "No one is more quickly forgotten in Washington," he told me once, "than a defeated politician." He had watched senators come and go over the past twenty-eight years. He himself had refused to go back to the Senate floor after his defeat, because he remembered how pathetic it was to see defeated senators haunting their old ground of power once their power was gone.

Church had never really been at home in Washington. As he confessed once to a reporter in 1974, "I've been here eighteen years and I have no feeling of belonging to this city." Senator Joseph Biden of Delaware acknowledged the same thing about Church from a somewhat different perspective. Recalling that Church had stayed up until the early morning hours drinking coffee in Biden's kitchen, consoling him when his wife and daughter were killed in an accident, Biden said, "Some of the very things he is criticized for in this town are some of the things this town secretly admires the hell out of. Frank Church has come to Washington, and has become one of the most important men in the country and in the world . . . and Frank Church still loves his wife, Frank Church still lives in a modest home, Frank Church doesn't put on airs about that kind of thing. The kind of airs Frank Church puts on are the product of his intellectual superiority. They are not airs. They are him."

On one of my visits in early March, Dad gathered the family around and we made plans for his funeral and burial. At first, he insisted that there be only one service, and that it be held in Boise. "I see no point of having a memorial service in Washington," he said.

We disagreed. "Think of all the friends who have been calling and visiting," I reminded him. "You may not want a service here, but they are going to need one." He reluctantly consented. "On one condition—" he said, "that we have it in a little chapel. I know from my days in politics that it is better to pack a small room than to leave a large one three-quarters empty." I said that we would do whatever was necessary. Two thousand people came to Frank Church's memorial service in the National Cathedral.

Between our initial conversation on this subject and his death, however, several things happened to reconcile Church to the fact that he might not be forgotten, even in Washington. As a token of what was to follow, Frank and Bethine returned home to find an article about them in the February issue of *The Washingtonian*. It was entitled, "What is this thing called love?" There is a wonderful picture of the two of them, and Bethine is quoted as saying, "We like to do everything together. We even sing in the car together—Frank's got the better voice, but I know the words."

More surprising to Church was an article by columnist David Broder, based on a conversation with Church in December, that ran in the Washington *Post* on January 22. It was entitled, "Frank Church's Challenge." Characteristically, it was an attack upon American foreign policy—this time in Latin America.

"Over the years," Broder wrote, "I had watched Church in some dramatic moments, during the civil rights debates in the 1950s, when he played a key role; in a Democratic convention keynote speech; an Idaho re-election campaign, and in his try for the Democratic presidential nomination in 1976. But sitting in his law office, interviewing Church for the first time since he lost his Senate seat in 1980, what I remembered was a dinner he organized for a group of reporters in a Capitol Hill restaurant in about 1964."

On that occasion, Church and Hans Morgenthau of the University of Chicago had arranged a dinner seminar concerning the danger of growing American involvement in Vietnam. The reporters were skeptical of Church's and Morgenthau's argument that the struggle taking place in Vietnam was not aggression by proxy from China or Moscow but an indigenous revolution; their point then was that, should we be so myopic as to ignore this and follow France in an attempt to halt this revolution by military intervention, we would surely pay a terrible price. Broder went home unconvinced. Over the next dozen years, however, he had many occasions to recollect Church's and Morgenthau's warning.

In December 1983, the subject was Central America. "The stupidity of it!" Church exclaimed. He spoke with such passion that Broder had trouble keeping up with his notes. "He knew that he was ill," Broder wrote, "and indicated in the conversation that it might be serious. But more than the gravity that fact imparted to his words, it was the recollection of the earlier occasion that gave them weight."

> "Remember," Church said, "how many years we pursued stupid policies in Asia, based on ignorance and an irrelevant ideological view of the world. . . . All those years of trying to 'contain' China, . . . and then we finally woke up one day and recognized the reality, through the eyes of two very unlikely witnesses, Richard Nixon and Henry Kissinger.
>
> "Yet we seem unable to learn from the failure of our Vietnam policy, or the equally evident failure of our hard-line policy toward Castro in Cuba. It is this idea that the Communist threat is everywhere that has made our government its captive and its victim.
>
> "Somehow, someday, this country has got to learn to live with revolution in the Third World. It's endemic. It's relatively easy to suppress revolution in Grenada, so we congratulate ourselves. It's more difficult to suppress it in Nicaragua or Central America, so we fret about that. But it will be impossible when it comes to Brazil or Argentina.
>
> "This country has become so conservative—so fearful —that we have come to see revolution anywhere in the world as a threat to the United States. It's nonsense. And yet that policy we have followed has cost us so many lives, so much treasure, such setbacks to our vital interests, as a great power ought not to endure.

"Until we learn to live with revolution, we will continue to blunder, and it will work to the Soviets' advantage. It will put them on the winning side, while we put ourselves on the side of rotten, corrupt regimes that end up losing.

"And each time one of those regimes is overthrown, it feeds the paranoia in this country about the spread of communism. It furthers the premise of the national security state, which means more militarism, more censorship, more spending, more deficits—and more casualties."

There was more, Broder said. "But I think those lines suggest the challenge Frank Church was raising. Considering the source—and the circumstances of his life—it is a challenge worth pondering."

Broder's piece awakened Frank Church. For a man who had been active in public affairs for thirty years, it is amazing how little confidence he had about his own place in history. "I am the messenger who brought the bad news," he said to me once. "Even if the king doesn't cut off his head, his name is conveniently forgotten."

Two weeks after David Broder's article appeared, Church agreed to write an essay on revolution for the Outlook section of the Washington *Post*. The two events together, Broder's piece and this invitation, were the beginning of Church's reconciliation with the Washington establishment.

My father had only two months more to live and he knew it. Even so, the prospect of making a valedictory statement of a lifetime's reflection upon American foreign policy gave him new life. He called me down from New York and brought in Jerry Levinson, of all Church's advisers the one who was most sympathetically conversant with Church's iconoclastic views, and the three of us sat down and began to sketch out the article.

My father thought he would need my help, but he did

not. For days, in almost every free moment, he penned his thoughts on a yellow pad or read them into a dictaphone. Jerry would take them and work them into draft form. Dissatisfied, my father revised the copy again and again. For three weeks, every time I came down to Washington, this article was foremost on his mind. Finally, he finished it. On March 11, in the Sunday Outlook section of the Washington *Post*, Church's article, "We Must Learn to Live With Revolutions," appeared.

Church began by citing our own revolution. The reason that we failed to learn from it was that it was essentially a revolt against political stupidity and insensitivity. We never had to deal with the limitless misery of an impoverished minority. "Our experience is alien to other countries which do not share our natural wealth," Church wrote. "In poor countries a desperate majority often lives on the margin of subsistence. A selfish property-owning minority and, often, an indifferent middle class intransigently protect their privileges. Dissidence is considered subversive. It isn't surprising that those who seek change resort to insurrection."

Church argued that revolutions are not romantic, simply inevitable. The fact that they are inevitable need not mean disaster for the United States, however. If we could somehow learn to live with revolution, the revolutionary governments, once in power, would have a much more favorable attitude toward us. Only by resisting the inevitable do we force the revolutionaries into the arms of the Soviets.

> The problem is illustrated in human terms by a vignette of the Kissinger Commission in Nicaragua [Church wrote]. According to press accounts, the members of the commission were angered by the confrontational tone of the meeting with the Nicaraguans and their obvious reliance on Soviet and Cuban intelligence.

Imagine the setting: the commission arrives in Nicaragua one week after the *contras*, supported by the United States, blow up a major oil facility. On the one side, a largely conservative commission led by Henry Kissinger, Robert Strauss, William Clements and Lane Kirkland, men in their late 50s or 60s, expecting to be acclaimed for their willingness to listen to the upstart revolutionaries. On the other side, peacock-proud Nicaraguan *commandantes* in their 30s or early 40s, men and women who had spent years fighting in the mountains, who had seen their friends and comrades die at their side in opposition to the U.S.-supported Somoza dictatorship, and naturally resentful of U.S. support of the counterrevolution. To them, a commission led by Kissinger, architect of the campaign to destabilize Allende, had to be seen as a facade for the American plan to bring them down. Is it a wonder there was no meeting of minds?

As I proofread this article, I thought back upon my estrangement from my father during the Vietnam period. Now, here I was, the minister of a comfortable, slightly liberal but clearly mainstream establishment New York City congregation. I was in my thirties. My father was almost sixty and about to die. Of the two of us, he was the radical now. I had to wonder to myself if, in the most important ways, he had not always been.

The final two months of Frank Church's life were filled with moments of recognition and reconciliation. Senator James McClure of Idaho, who had vigorously opposed its establishment, introduced legislation that the River of No Return Wilderness Area in Idaho be renamed the Frank Church–River of No Return Wilderness. Church was delighted. It was not Mount Borah, but, as Bill Hall, editor of the Lewiston *Morning Tribune*, wrote on March 18, "as puny pedestals go, the new 2.2-million-acre Frank Church–River of No Return Wilderness has its moments."

Part of its moment had to do with McClure's own gracious, if politically astute, shepherding of this bill into law during Frank Church's last days. My father said to me in late March, "I was a bit hasty in my dismissal of your eulogy, Forrest. Now, with Broder's column and this wilderness bill I have also read my obituary and seen my monument. There are certain advantages to dying slowly."

Once, years before, my father had told me that his chosen way to die would be a massive heart attack. "One moment I would be walking down the street playing with a thought, the next moment I would be dead." What he feared most, and secretly expected, was a recurrence of cancer.

Fortunately, we are not in charge of our own destiny. Though Frank Church was a man at peace with himself, during the final months of his life he was able to make a closure that in certain tangible ways was redemptive. He was quite surprised by the outpouring of affection. He discovered that people held him in esteem not only in Idaho but also in Washington and all around the country. For one whose only belief in immortality was cached in the bank of personal and historical memory, this knowledge was sustaining.

We, his family and friends, needed this time more than my father did. It gave us an opportunity again to say how much we loved him. And it provided us with one more chance to learn something important from him. As I said at his funeral in Boise, not only did my father teach us how to live, he also taught us how to die.

The decision to keep my father at home, without any life supports and in his own bed was, in our case, certainly the right decision. So often we die in unnatural surroundings. Most of us die in antiseptic environments, surrounded by strangers and attached to machines. Fortunately, increasingly more is being done within the medical community to humanize hospitals and to make it possible for more people to die with dignity. Even so, unlike in earlier centuries, our image of death is strongly colored by the feelings of estrangement and fear that so many of us feel when a loved one's life is invasively, if often impressively, fought for by people for whom death represents failure and the prolongation of life, however diminished, a triumph.

Many of us, of course, would not be alive today were it not for the miracle of modern medicine and the devotion of its practitioners. It is simply that one casualty of the modern age is that most of us are distanced as never before from the experience of death. The most natural thing in the world has become a taboo.

Church himself was typically wry on the subject. "Do you know why great men die well?" my father asked me one day about two weeks before his death. "Because it is expected of them," he said.

At one level this is true. A public person does often have to die a public death. His or her public watches, if only from a distance, some seeking perhaps a strange form of voyeuristic satisfaction, others a glint of illumination to guide them on their own dark way. Daily the reporters would call our home. Visitors would be quizzed on "the senator's spirits," or "what he had for breakfast." For one who has played a role on the public stage all his or her life, death becomes a finale. Whether you have known and loved these people all your life, or know them only as interchangeable faces in the crowd, you don't want to let your public down.

Frank Church didn't. Until the day before he died, whenever there were visitors he rose to the occasion. Finally, he could barely speak, but the last thing to go was his incandescent smile.

Before he lost his strength, Church would regale his visitors with stories. One he particularly enjoyed was the story of the old Indian chief who went into the mountains to die. His time had come. He ceremonially handed over his symbols of power, and bade farewell to his family and friends. When all of the farewell festivities were completed, he took his bedroll and climbed to a favorite spot of his in the mountains. There the old chief fixed his bed, lay down, folded his hands across his chest, and prepared to die. Finally he drifted off, only to be awakened some hours later by a rainstorm. Not being able to stand it any longer, he cursed under his breath, picked up his blanket, and returned, embarrassed and chagrined, to his tribe. "If I take my blanket and move toward the porch one of these nights," my father said, "will one of you please be sure to throw a little water on my head?"

Church's last meetings with people were almost always memorable. His dear friend George McGovern came by on the Tuesday before Church died. "He was too weak to speak, except for a word or two, but was still attempting to smile," McGovern said at the memorial service in Washington. "I have always felt awkward in embracing another man, but I found myself leaning over and holding him in my arms, believing that he was asleep. But he whispered in my ear, 'You are a dear man.' I simply could not speak at that moment, but I'm going to say now, 'Frank, you are the dear man.'"

I had left on Tuesday morning but came back early Thursday upon learning that my father's condition was much worse. I arrived at the house at about eight thirty in the morning. Ted Kennedy was at my father's bedside. It became clear to me throughout my father's illness that Kennedy is a man who understands death and dying. He had fulfilled his obligations to my father long before, but Kennedy kept coming back, all by himself, early in the morning or after work, just to sit quietly at my father's bedside. He talked about his nieces and nephews, wanted to hear about Nina and Twig, and in saying good-bye told my father that he was the conscience of the Senate and was deeply missed.

Kennedy spoke at the memorial service also. On his final visit with Frank Church, Kennedy recalled, "He opened his eyes, looked up and said, 'I think it's coming soon.' He smiled, and I think I know why he flashed that famous smile then. I believe he chuckled that morning because he knew the best orator of our time in the Senate would not be available for this service, so he was asking some of the rest of us to do the best we could."

I do not want to romanticize my father's death. It was hard. He was in considerable pain, and during the last three weeks of his life he became increasingly impatient with efforts to feed him or lift his spirits. He had no appetite. There were times when he resented being cajoled. About a week before he died, at a particularly dark moment, he said to my mother, "The worst thing about all this is that you can grow to hate the people you love the most."

From that point on, Bethine stopped all attempts to feed him or to make him do anything he did not want to do. She told him that she was ready for him to go. She told him that she wanted what he then so desperately wanted. She too wanted him to die. Mother asked Amy and Chase and me to give him our release also. He seemed grateful and relieved.

The last real conversation Frank Church had was on Friday morning, when our cousin John Church came by to pay his last respects. "How are you doing, Frank—I mean spiritually?" John asked. Frank Church opened his eyes, looked at his cousin, and simply said, "John, it is very, very interesting."

I was of little help to my father spiritually in his final days. I discovered that it is almost impossible to be a son and a minister at the same time. I could not gather either the strength or the presumption to speak intimately to my father about death.

Friday, the day before Frank Church died, was excruciatingly long. The house was filled with friends, neighbors, and loved ones. My father was only half-conscious and in considerable pain. The day before we had given him morphine for the first time. As the day wore on, his breathing became more labored. It was painful to be with him, and painful to be apart.

By about ten o'clock in the evening, my father was in great discomfort. I called Mary McCabe, the head nurse of the Vince Lombardi Cancer Center, at home, and she got in touch with the medical director, Dr. Charles Wooley. By 11 PM she had arrived with stronger doses of morphine and syringes. She gave my father an injection and then showed my mother how to do the same.

By midnight the doctor arrived. He stayed for about an hour, spending much of the time standing in silence at my father's bedside. I went upstairs to join him, and thanked him for his care and for all the comfort he had given my parents. "I just lost my own father earlier this year," he said to me. "It has changed me, not only as a man but as a doctor. Such times as these are so important. Your parents are both amazing people. I was dubious about the senator's dying at home, but I have learned something from this. We could have prolonged his life for two or three weeks, but knowing your parents, I see now that it would not have been right. Your mother has been incredible. You should be very proud of her, of both of them." There were tears in his eyes. He cried openly when he said good-bye.

I stayed up talking with Peter Fenn and Cleve Corlett, my father's old press secretary, until the early hours of the morning. Finally, at about two thirty, they went home and I to bed.

My wife could not sleep. After tossing about a bit, she

went downstairs to read. My mother saw the light on and called Amy up to my parents' room. There the three of them lay, together in bed until dawn. Amy and my mother talked quietly. My mother would alternately stroke my father's hand and rub Amy's back. "He's about to go," she said to Amy at seven in the morning. They opened the curtains and Amy returned to our room. At fifteen of eight on Saturday, April 7, 1984, my father died. My mother came into our room and said simply, "Dad is gone."

Almost at once, the house was buzzing with a welter of activity. The whole family gathered, and dozens of old friends, neighbors, and staffers arrived to be with my mother and with one another. Washington friends brought food and drink. Steve Emerson led us in the Kaddish prayer. Marian Burros arrived and took over the food preparation. My father was dead, but our house was alive with stories and laughter.

One story my father would have loved. Bethine and Chase went to the funeral home to pick a casket. They wanted a simple wooden one, and the undertaker obliged by beginning with the top of his line. "Something a little more simple than that," my mother kept saying, until they finally found one she liked, the least expensive wooden casket in the house.

"It is poplar, you know," the undertaker cautioned.

"Oh," Bethine Church replied, "Frank loved poplar. There are so many stands of poplar in Idaho."

"Ma'am, poplar grows everywhere," replied the undertaker. "It is a very common tree. Wouldn't you like to consider this simple walnut casket for the senator? It's a little more masculine."

As my brother reported when they came home, tears of laughter streaming down his face, "Do you want to know how much more masculine? I'll tell you exactly. It was four hundred dollars more masculine—that's how masculine it was!"

On Sunday morning I tried to go to church. I went to the Cedar Lane Unitarian Church in Bethesda. A water main had burst the night before, and services were canceled. When I returned home, I found my mother with Secretary and Mrs. Muskie, and two other old friends from my father's Senate days, Abigail McCarthy and Barbara Eagleton. They too had just come from church, a Catholic church in Bethesda. The priest's sermon had been about my father. We got calls throughout the weekend, indicating that the same was true in many churches and synagogues across the country.

Sunday's paper was filled with news of the secret CIA war against Nicaragua, and the mining of the Managua harbor. The connection between this and Senator Church's death was noted by several columnists. "The death of Frank Church . . . was a sad ending to a traumatic week, a painful reminder of how few can say no to a president and call an outlaw government agency to account," wrote Mary McGrory in the Washington *Post*. Noting that thirteen "warrior-Democrats" in the Senate had joined their Republican colleagues in voting the continuation of covert aid to the Nicaraguan *contras*, McGrory said that Church "will be remembered when they are long forgotten, as a gentle, honorable man who voted his principles rather than his fears."

Anthony Lewis, also reflecting upon the juxtaposition of Church's death and U.S. efforts in Nicaragua, wrote in *The New York Times* that "the lesson is plain enough. In dealing with revolutionary governments, the strength of the United States does not lie in war, covert or otherwise. It lies in the open economy—and the open society. . . . Some of us yearn, with Frank Church, for the day 'we stop trying to repress the irrepressible and exchange our unreasonable fear of Communism for a rekindled faith in freedom.' "

On Monday morning, I met with Bishop Bill Spofford, an old friend from Idaho, now serving at the National

Cathedral as auxiliary bishop of Washington. He could not have been more gracious or accommodating. The service was held on Tuesday morning. My father had asked Senators Kennedy and McGovern, former Secretary of the Interior Cecil Andrus, and me to speak. Senator Claiborne Pell, another close friend, gave the reading. We chose 1 Corinthians 13, Paul's definition of love.

The cathedral was packed with people: friends and neighbors, former staffers, people from my congregation in New York, a contingent from Gettysburg, Pennsylvania, several of my old high school and college friends, dozens of senators and congressmen. Representatives were also in attendance from almost every embassy in Washington. It was the day of the First Lady's congressional wives' luncheon, which she graciously agreed to postpone so that my mother's many friends could be with her. They all came.

Mrs. George Bush was there representing the White House. Senator and Mrs. Gary Hart interrupted their campaigning in Pennsylvania, as did Mrs. Walter Mondale. My mother was particularly pleased to see Lady Bird Johnson.

It must have been very hard for Mrs. Johnson. Everyone mentioned Church's opposition to the President on Vietnam. Senator Kennedy said, "Frank Church was among the first lonely voices of dissent raised in the wilderness of warmaking in Vietnam. He was a senator from Idaho; but he was also a voice for those half a world away who had no votes to cast against the bombing and devastation of their own land." George McGovern too recalled their joint struggle against the war: "Once after a lopsided Senate vote against one of our joint ventures, I saw Frank ambling across the Senate floor with an amused expression on his face. 'George,' he said, 'I've learned two things about this partnership of ours. We're always right, but we always lose!'

176

"Whether in fact we were right or wrong," McGovern said, "history will decide, but I shall always feel that Frank Church was a witness to the world for what is decent and just in human affairs—one of the great senators in American history. In Lincoln's phrase, he always appealed to the 'better angels of our nature.' "

I spoke for Chase and myself. "As we look back upon our upbringing, one really quite extraordinary thing strikes home. Never did we sense that we were growing up in the household of a great man. We grew up in the household of a great father."

I recalled his generous accession to my wedding vows at a time when my proclamation of pacifism complicated his own efforts to end the war. And I cited the way in which he and my mother responded to Chase's passion for open spaces by renting a cabin to spend weekends in Pennsylvania, thus reaffirming a sense of priorities that many of us lose track of.

"One last thing," I closed by saying. "And this is the hardest thing for me to say, because there is so much pain in it. It is the kind of pain we would pray for, if we had any sense, for that is the way love is. The more you love the more you risk to lose. My father and my mother together were one of the great American love stories. As great as most of us will ever know. He is gone now. I really don't have to say anything more."

On Wednesday morning about twenty of us—the immediate family, several old staff members, and a few close friends—flew to Idaho for my father's funeral. When we arrived in Boise, we were taken immediately to the Capitol Building, where Frank Church lay in state that night. There was a brief ceremony led by the governor. Over the next few hours thousands of people filed by Senator Church's casket.

On Thursday his funeral was held at the Cathedral of the Rockies. Again, the note of celebration and thanks-

177

giving rang clear. As with the memorial service in Washington, the tone was set by Thornton Wilder's words quoted on the memorial program: "All that we can know about those we have loved and lost is that they would wish us to remember them with a more intensified realization of their reality. What is essential does not die but clarifies. The highest tribute to the dead is not grief but gratitude."

In my own remarks I said, "In a very real way, this celebration of my father's life is a family celebration. For you are family too. Dad thought of you that way. It is not just that so many of you care, as my father so deeply cared, about the quality of life, the preservation of our environment, the establishment of a just and compassionate society, the struggle for peace. Transcending each of these, this is a family celebration because my father had, and lived by, a profound sense of the kinship of all people. We share the same home, this beautiful, fragile planet earth. We share the same fate. We are mysteriously given life, and for a brief time blessed with opportunities to love and serve and forgive one another as best we can. We are gifted with special powers for good, each of us is. My father devoted much of his life to helping us, individually and collectively, to realize and act upon these powers, not to settle for who we are, but to stretch and become who we might be. In so many wondrous ways, my father taught us how to live.

"He also taught us how to die," I said in closing. "I have never seen or known a man who was less afraid of death. If religion is our human response to the dual reality of being alive and having to die, my father, from a very early age, was touched with natural grace. Because my father was not afraid to die, he was not afraid to live. He did not spend his life, as so many of us do, little by little until he was gone. He gave it away to others. He invested it in things that would ennoble and outlast him.

In his life, my father was a bit like the day star, rising early to prominence, brilliant in the dusk and against the darkness, showing other stars the way. When it came time for him to go, when his precious flame flickered, he was ready. Peacefully, naturally, with serenity and grace, he returned his light unto the eternal horizon. Like the day star, my father went out with the dawn."

My five-year-old son, Twig, was there at the service for his grandfather that beautiful spring day. Twig and I have often sat down together to talk since then. We have talked about death, about his grandfather, and about God. Nina too talks often of her Opa, and as she grows older she will fashion her own questions about death and God. As for now, she says simply that when she grows up she wants to be God, because God never dies.

It is now summer's end. My father has been dead for almost five months. One chapter closes and another begins. Tomorrow I leave Boston for New York City to begin my seventh year as minister of All Souls. Fortunately, others are writing the story of my father's life. They will bring insight and detail to this task that I could not. What I did bring was myself and that part of my father that is in me.

Epilogue

Two weeks after my father died, I had a new-member appointment with an engaging woman about my age, exactly half the proverbial three-score and ten. Her daughter and mine had just turned three. They are classmates during the week and at the church school on Sundays. We first met two and a half years ago, when she and her husband called upon me to christen their daughter.

Near the end of our discussion, she asked me a question that I had a hard time answering. One of the reasons it was such a difficult question is that it came from her daughter. Children often ask better, harder, more important questions than we adults do. It is not their fault. They don't know any better.

In any event, this little girl asked her mother to tell her where she had been before she started growing in her mommy's tummy. I hasten to add that this little girl's mother did the sensible thing. She punted in hope for better field position on a later set of downs. She sat her daughter down and said, "That is a very good and very hard question, honey. I will think about it carefully, and then come back with an answer a little later." What she then did was a very rational, if unreasonable, thing to do. She went to her library, took out a book called *The Magic Years*, and started searching for clues.

Our children have a great, if unwarranted, sense of confidence in us, and this little story continues to demonstrate both sides of that equation.

"What are you doing, Mommy?"

"I am looking for the answer to your very good, very hard question," her mother replied.

If you do not have this book in your library, and are interested in the answer to this question, I can tell you that you will not find it there or in any book. For the little girl, however, the book became very important. Later that evening her father found her reading it upside down in the bathroom.

"What are you doing, sweetheart?"

"Mommy told me that I can find out where I was before I was born by looking in this book. But, Daddy," she said, "there aren't any pictures." At which point, as if I didn't have enough impertinent children of my own, this little girl's parents resolved to come to me in search of an acceptable answer.

Two days later, I was visiting one of our long-time members, a gentle, lovely woman, who has been a member of All Souls for almost fifty years and was in the hospital. We had a wonderful conversation. She was in good spirits, and, given how much trouble she had been having lately, looked hale and beautiful to me. After our conversation had gone along for a while, she asked me, "Forrest, what do you think happens to us after we die?"

At that very moment it struck me. Not the answer, exactly. I really don't know the answer to that question. What struck me was that the two questions, hers and that of the little girl, were very much the same. "Where were we before we were born?" "What happens to us after we die?" One is an important, existential question for the very young; the other an important, existential question for those of us who are nearing the end of our lives. I thought about my own age, almost exactly halfway between that of this bright little girl and this strong and wise older woman. Weighing the questions one against the other, I felt deep within a balance point between them. Where am I? Am I halfway between nothing and nothing? Or something and something? Or everything and everything?

To begin with, it strikes me that of all that we experience, there is nothing more natural than birth and death. Nothing that happens between can even begin to approximate either birth or death in terms of absolute unadulterated naturalness. Birth and death are spontaneous acts, not conscious ones. They are perfect acts of nature. We know this about birth, I think, but death is somewhat different. One of the reasons that death is different is that we are conscious of it in advance and are frightened by it.

Looking at this in a purely biological way, however, without death there would be no birth, not as we know it, for the simplest forms of life never die. For all practical purposes, they are immortal. French scientist Lecomte du Nouy put it this way:

> The cell or the organism separates into two [like organisms] which live, grow, and in their turn each separate into two others. They never die, except accidentally. ... Asexual cells do not know death as individuals. They are immortal. All of a sudden, with sexual generation we see the appearance of an entirely new and unforeseen cyclical phenomenon: the birth and death of the individual. [Accordingly] ... we can say that from an evolutionary point of view the greatest invention of Nature is death.

In other words, we were immortal until we became interesting! On the one hand, this invites us to reconsider the advantages of immortality. Because we die, we are privileged to be born. On the other hand, far from persuading us to disbelieve in immortality, this same observation challenges us to think about immortality in new, more dynamic, less selfish terms.

Before I do, let me take all of this one step further. For me it is a sufficient step. It is one of the reasons that I don't worry all that much about where I was before I was born and where I will be after I die. It is not that these are unimportant questions. It is just that for me the miracle lies in between. No experience of being, unknown to us and probably unknowable, that has taken place before this life or will take place after it, could possibly be more remarkable, more wonderful, or more strange than this life we share today. Life is a miracle couched between mysteries. It is a miracle incarnate, not a given, but a gift, an unaccountable gift. When we take it for granted, or beg for something more, we do it violence.

Nonetheless, these questions remain and they are not unimportant ones. So let me hazard an answer to each. My guess—and it is no more than a guess—is this. Before we are born and after we die, we are with God. We come from God, spend a lifetime imperfectly manifesting the promise of God incarnate as God-carriers, and then return to God when we die.

Admittedly, I have an unorthodox view of God, one I cannot prove. Nor would I even want to try. For me, God is the genius of the life force, that which is greater than all and yet present in each. Try as I will, I simply cannot explain or understand the miracle of life, and, yes, of birth and death, in any other way. God is not God's name. God is our name for the spirit that animates and impels and finally infolds our lives into its own. I don't anticipate that I, as a distinct individual, will be any more conscious of God, or of my participation in God, after I die than I was before I was born. All I know is that the miracle we participate in daily, this miracle of

breathing, and thinking, and acting, and failing, and loving and dying, is not wholly accidental. Neither is it
discrete, bounded by a distinct and absolute beginning
and ending. We are a part of something larger, something ongoing and eternal, inscrutable perhaps even
unto itself. The more I contemplate all of this, by the
way, the more reverent I become, the more undemand-
ing of final answers, the more accepting of all that was
and of all that will be.

When I was a little boy I believed in God without
questioning what I really meant by this. God was God
and that was that. Far more important than the existence
of God was that of the goblins and evil spirits that lurked
under my bed at night. About them I knew at least this
much. When my mother turned on the light, got on her
hands and knees, raised the bedspread, and looked under
the bed, they were gone. When she turned off the light
and left the room, they returned in force to haunt me.

In my early years God figured in precisely the opposite fashion. When things were going well, when I did
not need God, God was there. I believed in God without
worrying much about why. When darkness fell and I
was troubled, when I experienced what in later years
would recur periodically as a dark night of the soul, I
could not sense God anywhere.

So it was that I decided that if God did exist, God was
not important to me. Other things were infinitely more
important. I believed in what I could see, what I could
touch, what I could learn. Compared with these, the
wonders of a distant God in heaven held no allure. I
guess I found myself believing in the rainbow but not in
the pot of gold at the end of it. If it did exist, it was not
important to me. Or, more precisely, I knew enough, or
thought I did, not to search for it, for such a search would
be in vain. By the time I closed in, the rainbow would
be gone.

None of this has changed. I still believe in the vanishing rainbow as I do in the dark sky over the mountains. But I also believe in God, and I believe that God is important to me. The God I believe in now is different from the God I did not believe in then.

The God I believe in now does not intercede, like a royal eagle swooping down from on high, to save the day for those who, outnumbered and outflanked, fight under God's banner. The God I believe in is not bothered in the least by the lack of prayer in the public schools. Pray for rain and the God I believe in will not answer, whatever the change in the weather. And it makes no difference who is doing the praying, for the God I believe in does not play favorites when it comes to faith or creed. The God I believe in is not male or female or any divine combination of the two. All this I know or think I know. On the other hand, I do not know, and think I never will know, just what the God I believe in is. The God I believe in remains a mystery to me. It is hard to put in words, but let me close by sharing with you my own experience of the mystery of God.

If my theology, that is, my way of thinking about God, is grounded anywhere, it would be upon the principles of humility and openness. As to the first of these, and it may be a truism, the more I know of life and death and love, the greater my ignorance appears. Beyond every ridge lies another slope and beyond every promontory looms yet another vast and awesome range. However far we trek, while cursed (or blessed) with the knowledge of our own mortality, we shall never finally know the answer to the question why. This, by the way, is one of the reasons I cannot embrace a dogmatic faith. Even should the dogma be fashioned wholly according to my own liking, experience tells me that it would not stand the test, my own test, of growth, unfolding truth, and time. This, then, is the lesson of humility. Alone it is insuffi-

Humility

186

cient, teaching us only what we cannot hope to know. On the other hand, openness, the possibility principle, invites us to probe life as deeply as we can, without regard to limits. So it is that, accepting my smallness while remaining open to explore as fully as possible the unresolvable mystery of my own and our shared being, I find myself growing in faith. The mystery of life becomes ever more deep and wondrous, the gift of life ever more precious and unaccountable. By remaining open to the unknown, one dares to enter further into it. One grows in knowledge—yes, and in ignorance—but one also grows in wonder and, finally, in trust.

My own forays are usually journeys taken in meditation or prayer, but they also may come about through the medium of music, or nature, or some magical moment of human interaction. Losing oneself one finds oneself, and one's whole perspective is changed.

Here words begin to fail me. I can only describe the experience as one of mystical union in that which is greater than all of its parts and yet present in each, that which gives meaning to all, beyond explanation, beyond knowing or naming. This power which I cannot explain or know or name I call God. God is not God's name. God is our name for the mystery that wells within and looms beyond the limits of our being. Life force, spirit of life, ground of being, these too are names for the unnameable which I am now content to call my God.

When I pray to God, God's answer to me comes from within and not from beyond. God's answer is *Yes*, not to the specifics of my prayer, but in response to my hunger for meaning and peace. God's answer is not a what or a how or a when but a yes. *Choose life and trust life. Grow in service and in love. Take nothing for granted. Be thankful for the gift. Suffer well. Dare to risk much. Consecrate your world with laughter and with tears. And know not what I am or who*

Yes!

I am or how I am, know only that I am with you. This is God's answer to my prayers.

As I plunge deeper, in fits and starts, seeking to penetrate the mystery of God, the mystery grows. It grows in wonder and in power, in moment and in depth. There are times of distraction, fragmentation, alienation, and brokenness when God is not with me. But when I open myself to God, my wholeness is restored.

Perhaps that which I call the mystery of God is no more than the mystery of life itself. I cannot know, nor do I care, for the power that emanates from deep within the heart of this mystery is redemptive. It is divine. By opening myself to it, without ever hoping or presuming to understand it, I find peace.

The mystery of God will remain a mystery. That, I suppose, is as it should be. Anything less would fail to do justice to the miracle of consciousness, of love and of pain, of life and of death. Responding to this miracle, responding to God's _Yes_, and, especially, in offering my thanks for the gift of my father's life, I can do no other than to answer "Yes" in return. "Yes, I place my trust in Thee. Yes, I offer up my heartfelt thanks."

Index

Index

191

Index

Ramsbotham, Sir Peter, 45
Reagan, Ronald, 142, 144, 145, 149
Reeves, Beulah, 162
Richardson, Elliot, 45
Right-wing religious groups, 143–145
River of No Return Wilderness, 73.
    See also Frank Church–River of
    No Return Wilderness
River Road Unitarian Church, 129
Robinson Bar Ranch, 20, 21, 33, 73
Rockefeller, Nelson, 102, 103
Rockwell, Hays, 132
Rodino, Peter, 120
Rood, Wayne, 84
Roosevelt, Eleanor, 11
Roosevelt, Franklin D., 17, 22, 36
Roper, Elmo, 53
Rostow, Walt, 125

St. Augustine, 68
Salt II Treaty, 139–141
Saturday Evening Post, 27
Schmitz, John, 95
Schneider, René, 104
Senate Foreign Relations
    Committee, 9, 18, 51, 57, 90, 108,
    133–135, 139, 140
Senate Intelligence Committee, 37
Senate Interior Committee, 72
Senate Select Committee on
    Intelligence, 101–106, 122
Simpson, Alan, 155
Smith, Robert, 96
Soviet Union, 58, 100, 136, 138–141
Space program, 83
Sparkman, John, 133, 136
Spofford, Bishop Bill, 175, 176
Spingarn, Natalie Davis, 158
Stanford Law School, 33, 84
Stanford Medical Center, 7
Stanford University, 6, 23, 63, 64, 76
Stang, Alan, 95
Stars and Stripes, 79
Stendahl, Krister, 151
Stevens, Roger, 53
Stevenson, Adlai, 36, 53, 54, 58
Stevenson, Adlai, III, 119
Stewart, Potter, 45
Stone, Senator, 139
"Studies in the History of
    Christian Thought," 93
Subcommittee on Multinational
    Corporations, 100, 101, 136
Symms, Steven, 96, 141, 156

Taylor, Glen, 35, 36
Theta Xi, 64–67
This Week, 53
Thomas, Dr. Lewis, 158
Thurmond, Strom, 52
Time, 53, 113, 114
Tower, John, 104
Trujillo, Rafael, 102, 104
Truman, Harry S., 23
Tussman, Major, 28

Udall, Morris, 111, 119
Unitarianism, 39, 97–99
United Fruit, 100
United Nations, 58
University of California, 86
University of Chicago, 164
U.S. Government Code, 87
U.S.-Soviet negotiations, 58

Valenti, Jack, 62
Vance, Cyrus, 139, 140
Vietnam, 9, 25, 59–62, 70, 71, 75, 77,
    95, 106, 164, 176
Village Voice, 61
Vince Lombardi Cancer Center, 173

Wallace, Henry, 22, 35
Ward, Porter, 37
Washingtonian, The, 164
Washington *Post*, 108, 116, 164, 167,
    175
Washington *Star*, 106
Welch, Mr., 53
Welker, Herman, 35–37
Wellington, Mr., 53
"What is this thing called love?"
    164
Whelan, Gerald, 114
Whitman and Ransom, 147, 148
Wild and Scenic Rivers Act, 72
Wilder, Thornton, 178
Wilderness Act, 72
Williams, George Huntston, 93, 97,
    99, 100, 124, 158
Williams, Rhys, 129
Wooley, Dr. Charles, 173
World War II, 25
Wright, Mr., 53

Yale Divinity School, 91, 92
Young, Andrew, 156
Young, Patsy, 162

193

ABOUT THE AUTHOR

F. Forrester Church has served as minister of All Souls
Unitarian Church in New York City since 1978, the same
year he received his Ph.D. from Harvard University. He
also holds a bachelor's degree in history from Stamford
and a divinity degree from the Harvard Divinity School.

Dr. Church was selected by *Esquire* magazine in 1984
as one of the outstanding Americans under forty.

He and his wife Amy have been married since 1970.
They have two children, Frank, six, and Nina, three.